The Secrets of

Successful Parenting

Understand what your child's behaviour is really telling you

Andrea Clifford-Poston

PATHWAYS

First published in 2001 by
How To Books Ltd, 3 Newtec Place,
Magdalen Road, Oxford OX4 1RE, United Kingdom
Tel: 01865 798306 Fax: 01865 248780

British Library Cataloguing in Publication Data
A catalogue record for this book is available from
the British Library

Edited by Diana Brueton
Cover design by Shireen Nathoo Design
Author photograph by Martin Rice

Produced for How To Books by Deer Park Productions
Typeset by PDQ Typesetting, Newcastle-under-Lyme
Printed and bound in Great Britain by Bell & Bain Ltd., Glasgow

Note: The material contained in this book is set out in good
faith for general guidance and no liability can be accepted for
loss or expenses incurred as a result of relying in particular
circumstances on statements made in the book. The laws and
regulations are complex and liable to change, and readers
should check the current position with the relevant
authorities before making personal arrangements.

Pathways is an imprint of
How To Books

Contents

Foreword   xi

Introduction   1
   A Sound Parental Instinct?   4
   Knowing and Not Knowing   6
   'Being Good with Kids'   7
   On Being the Expert   8
   So Where Do We Learn to Parent?   9
   If You Are a Single Parent   10
   A Soft Option?   10
   'For Now Sits Expectation in the Air'   12

1   Great Expectations – How Children Change Our Lives   13
   The Best Laid Plans   13
   Social Expectations   14
   Creative Fulfilment   16
   The First Task of Parenting – Childhood as a Time of
     Conflict   18
   Surviving the Experts   19
   A Baby Brings a Couple Closer Together   21
   Giving Them What I Never Had   24
   Doing It Better than Our Parents   25
   And What If You Are a Single Parent?   27
   Disappointment and Envy – The Problem of the
     Child-Free Couple   29
   'We Thought It Would Be Fun'   29
   Summary   30

2   The Stealing of Crowns – Sibling Rivalry   32
   A Further Expectation – 'Someone to Play With'   32
   False Expectations – 'It's Me You're Angry With...'   33
   Is Sibling Rivalry Inevitable?   34
   The Importance of Spoiling   38
   Loving and Hating   39

If Your Child Asks to Go to Boarding School   42
'And Then She Gloats' – the Importance of Triumph   43
The Family Baby – How do You Feel When You Make a
   Mess of It?   44
Do You Provoke Jealousy – Whether You Mean to or Not?   47
Will They Grow Out of It?   48
Can the Only Child Have Sibling Rivalry?   49
What Does 'Attention Seeking Behaviour Mean?'   50
Summary   51

3   **Goldilocks and the Little Don Quixotes – Lying and
   Stealing**   52
'Only Adults Can Do It'   52
Living a Lie   53
Are All Lies the Same?   54
Lying Over Trivial Matters – a Developmental Stage   54
Boasting Lies – Lying about Experiences and Achievements   56
Lies that Explain How I Feel   59
Disassociated Lies – It Wasn't Me!   60
Stealing   62
A Shocking Solution   63
Who Has the Stealer Robbed?   64
'Mummy Has It All' – Stealing Because I'm Envious   65
An Extraordinary Problem   66
Summary   66

4   **When Words Fail – Bullying**   68
Adults Bully   68
An Ordinary Problem   69
'I Wanted Him to Feel as Bad as Me' – Passing on the Pain   71
Parent Bashing   72
Defiance is Important   74
'My Mum's in a Bate' – Mirroring Family Relationships   77
Co-operation or Submission?   79
The Aggressive Victim   80
If Your Child is Being Bullied   82
Summary   82

5 'Honey and Bitter Aloes?' – Schooling Problems   83
   First Encounter with the World   83
   Failure to Settle in School   85
   Control v. Communication?   86
   The Child Who Doesn't Learn   89
   But Where Does the Problem Lie?   91
   When Anxiety is Helpful   95
   Trying New Food – Just a Taste! – Preparing Children
      for School   95
   Home Time   97
   The Cult of Maternal Business   98
   Summary   99

6 Believing in Goodness – The Impact of Divorce   100
   A Shattered 'Secure Base'   101
   A Failed Relationship?   102
   What Shall We Tell the Children?   103
   'Particular to Thee' – the Unique Experience   106
   A Kind of Bereavement?   109
   When Daddy Doesn't Visit   111
   The Child as a Weapon   111
   The Stages of Development   112
   Social and Political Factors   116
   How Parents Can Help   117
   Sharing the Care – Coping with Two Homes   124
   Remarriage   126
   On Being Adult   127
   Believing in Goodness   128
   Summary   128

7 On Never Winning – A Word to Working Mothers
      and Fathers   131
   Change and Opportunity   131
   The Impact of Choice   132
   Just a Housewife – Should Mothers be Paid?   133
   Doing Neither Well   134
   Quality Time – or a Bag of Crisps?   135
   From the Child's Point of View   136
   There's Nothing Wrong with Not Coping   137
   On Planning to Be a Working Mother   138

A Beauty Queen with a Briefcase 139
Having Fun Together 140
Single Parents 141
Summary 141

References 143
Further reading 145
Useful addresses 147
Index 149

Acknowledgements

I have written this book and I take full responsibility for the views expressed in it. However, there is a sense in which I cannot call it 'my own'. It is born of thousands of conversations throughout my life, with family, friends, teachers, lecturers, supervisors, colleagues, students and pupils, and of course the families with whom I have worked. The field of literature, people in bus queues, on trains, taxi drivers have also made their contributions – the list is endless. I am grateful to them all for enriching my life and helping me to shape my ideas. Nevertheless, there are certain specific contributions to this book which must be acknowledged.

The idea for the book arose from a lecture given at Dunnanie School (Bedales Pre-Prep). I am grateful to Sarah Webster and her staff for their ongoing support and encouragement.

Sarah Adams, Veronica Austen, Cheryl Batt, Morris and Tina Clifford, Sarah Davis, Janice Finnimore, Lin Fitch, Liz George, Mandy Kelly, Jenny Marlow, Lorraine Marshall, Elizabeth Roach, Tessa Smith, Nick Weekes and Carey-Ann Young, have made valuable comments on early drafts of the book.

Penny Carter has typed and re-typed the manuscript. She has done so efficiently and professionally, meeting impossible deadlines with calm good humour.

Adam Philips, who kindly agreed to write the Foreword, has inspired, supported and encouraged me professionally and personally throughout the writing of this book. At times, the reader may discern his dazzling creativity playing hokey-cokey with the text.

My greatest debt is, of course, to the families who have allowed me to be part of their history for a while. They have kept alive my sense of awe at what it means to be a family. I have grown with each relationship, and they have taught me much.

Finally, I thank my husband, for his continuing struggles to understand my behaviour – although in doing so I realise I thank part of myself.

Andrea Clifford-Poston

Disclaimer

Wherever actual quotations and family stories have been used, permission has been sought and kindly granted. However, names, dates and any other factors affording recognition of individuals have been changed to protect confidentiality. Any similarity to any child, parent or family, alive or dead, is therefore purely coincidental. The ordinary problems of childhood are trans-generational and universal.

Foreword

The advantage of living in an Age of Experts is that there is a
great deal of useful, specialist knowledge about virtually
everything we do. The drawback is that we don't always know
where to find it or who we can trust. When it comes to
bringing up children – one of the most demanding and
essential things we ever do – this can be particularly troubling.
Everyone has had their first lesson in child-rearing as a child,
with the people who cared enough about them to bring them
up. And everyone brings from their own childhood their own
theories and strong feelings about what children do and don't
need, many of which they are quite unaware of. Then when
people become parents they are surrounded by information, as
though society is at once keen to be helpful and reassuring
about what is always something of a shock, but also perhaps
wary of people coming to their own conclusions about
something people have been doing for a very long time. It is
quite possible for a new parent to wonder who their child
belongs to: the state with its midwives and paediatricians, child
psychologists and teachers; or the family with its always
unusual history, and its great internal resource – the previous
generation.

What *The Secrets of Successful Parenting* shows is that we
don't have to choose – we can use what the best experts tell us,
and be surprised by just how much we already know; and we
don't have to be intimidated – we can use what we already
know to work out what else might be good for us. Andrea
Clifford-Poston who, as both a teacher and a child and family
therapist is unusually well qualified to speak about these things
has, in other words, written a book that is both immensely
(and fascinatingly) informative, and strangely evocative. It
brings back memories, whilst stimulating new thoughts. And
though it is alive to the very real difficulties of family life, it
never forgets that people's pleasure in each other's company is
the best reason for them to be together.

Everyone adores their children; that's the easy part. What many people find more difficult is liking them day by day, and finding an enjoyable way to live together with them. *The Secrets of Successful Parenting* shows us just how practical we can be by not giving up on – by being attentive to – the subtle intelligence of our emotional lives. Indeed, the 'secret' of the title refers to the fact that children (and therefore adults) are above all communicative; that their survival, and the quality of their life, depends upon their ways of letting people know what they need. But they depend on the adults to be more than willing to listen to what they have to say (a letter without an address is not a letter). And this means, as Clifford-Poston shows so vividly being able to bear the child's feelings. This involves a good deal of uncertainty – the child doesn't need its parents to be experts on child rearing, but just to be as attentive as they can be – and a certain amount of muddling through. Being a parent is not, as this book makes so clear, about getting it right, so much as it is about not fearing getting it wrong.

Perhaps one of the greatest virtues of Clifford-Poston's book is that, despite how much useful basic knowledge it contains, it never loses sight of the fact that every child, like every family, is something of an experiment. It is part of the spirit of her book to see this as worth celebrating. If this is (in the best sense) a self-help book with a sense of wonder, it is because the author knows things, and tells us what she knows, without ever being too knowing. She never makes us feel that to bring up our children well we really need to be her. Now that there is more information than ever before – with children, and the whole notion of parenting being studied as never before – we tend to think that it is only information that we need. In this book the reader will certainly find the clearest accounts of up-to-date theories of child development. But I think there is something else in this book that is more difficult to describe – more difficult to advertise – and that may be more important, especially in a book about children. And that is, the speaking voice you can hear in the written words on the page. Listening to this book as you read – and it is a book literally packed with helpful suggestions about what to do when – you can hear the spirited affection of the author's voice. And it is this tone of voice, which leaves us free to agree and disagree with her, that makes *The Secrets of Successful Parenting* so valuable. Between the questions it asks, and the examples it gives, there is plenty of space for the reader to think their own thoughts freely about what is, after all, an endlessly intriguing subject: how children grow up without realising what they are doing because someone is looking after them.

Adam Phillips

For Sean
who hears, even in the silence
and
with three cheers for
Murray N. Cox F.R.C.P.
(1931–1997),
who was 'a good thing'.

Introduction

'When we came to see you we thought there was a right way ... (of bringing up children) ... and we were doing it wrong. We expected you to tell us how to do it properly. At first we were angry when you didn't ... then we realised it didn't matter too much if we got it wrong, and then we began to think ...'

As you, the reader, open this book, I am aware of your expectations of me, the author. This book is born of expectations; parents' expectations of children, parents' expectations of me, children's expectations of parents, and my expectations of parents. What has made you read it? Was it bought purposefully as a result of a troubling child, or idly discovered as you browsed through a shop? Was it recommended by a friend, by a professional who hoped it would reassure, or speak to you in a helpful way? Was it left 'lying around' by someone else, and picked up in a solitary, bored moment? What are you expecting from it? And what will have to happen for you to feel your expectations have been fulfilled?

It is unlikely that all of this book will speak to everybody. Some parents will find it disappointing, if not frustrating. You can be sure that if this book is not to be disappointing, at some point you will have to suspend your expectations of it, and enter a neutral space between what you long to hear and what I might feel able to say. In this way you may be freed to think about whether the thoughts expressed enhance your parenting or not.

It is not my intention to provide 'the right way', or instant solutions to difficult child behaviours. What I hope to do is to provide an ambience in which we can think about children's behaviour together. Children have very limited ways of letting us know when they have a problem. If they do not have the language, of if they cannot formulate the problem, then they

1

are likely to use behaviour as a way of communicating with the adults! The problem is, children often choose behaviour which does not accurately illustrate their worry. Then the behaviour itself is perceived as difficult and inappropriate by the adult. For example, a 4-year old, hurt and angry by the arrival of a new baby in the family, is mistaken when he thinks that the way to regain his parents' affection is to hit the baby. A vicious circle develops.

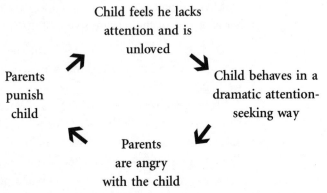

This book may differ from other books for parents in that it will focus less on how to control children's behaviour and more on how to understand it – the 'why' of children's behaviour. Once parents understand why a child is behaving the way he does, then very often they can come up with their own ways of controlling in a manner in which the child feels heard and understood – and consequently under less pressure to repeat inappropriate or undesirable behaviour. Parents are freed to put in place effective boundaries and discipline. The vicious circle can then be broken.

Child feels he lacks attention and is unloved
↓
Child behaves in dramatic
and attention-seeking way
↓
Parents understand child feels he lacks
attention and is unloved
↓
Parents help child to communicate
in a more appropriate way
↓
Child feels loved

A young mother came to see me distraught at the aggressive and demanding behaviour of her 3-year-old son. Her 5-year-old daughter suffered from cerebral palsy, and though not seriously disabled, needed more attention than most children of her age and was the focus of much anxiety and concern. Her little boy had become increasingly demanding over the previous six months and in the last few weeks had begun to lash out at both his mother and his sister, without provocation. The mother commented how he would sometimes stare intently at her after one of these aggressive outbursts, almost waiting to see what effect it had had on her. For some time the mother described the child's behaviour in a bewildered and confused manner. Eventually I asked her, 'How would James know when he'd made an impact on you?' She looked startled. She was silent for a moment and then her face lit up with relief, 'Well that's it, that's just what it feels like, he's trying to make an impact!' She was able to realise quickly perhaps how difficult the little boy found it to compete for attention with his sister – attention in the sense of preoccupying mummy's thoughts. With still a limited vocabulary he was unable to verbalise his anxieties and was resorting to behaviour – which certainly provoked a result!

Most parents desperately want to do their best as parents and are bewildered, confused and hurt when in spite of doing their best, things seem to go 'wrong'. I know from my clinical experience that parents have the potential to understand and manage the most complicated of situations and communications. However, in the hurly burly of daily life it is not surprising if sometimes they need someone to facilitate them in their task. A relative or friend may very often take on this role, but when 'an ordinary problem' of childhood becomes 'extraordinary', then professional help may be sought. Parents may arrive in the consulting room feeling guilty that they have failed and anxious that 'there is something wrong' with them or their child. Very rarely is that likely to be the case, most families who seek my help have simply got into a muddle. My job is to help them understand this muddle.

James' story is typical of both my work and the aim of this book – to describe situations in such a way that parents are enabled to handle the child in a way that they feel right. James' mother's reaction of 'put like that, it's obvious, of course it makes sense', is typical of many parents in a consultation. Therapy is not about correcting 'bad parenting', but more about thinking about parenting in a three-dimensional way. Sailing readers will understand that it is rather like forecasting the weather. This is most commonly done as a two-dimensional phenomenon, i.e. how we experience it on land or water, and the way it is seen on surface charts. However, the weather we experience is at the bottom of the Earth's atmosphere. It is greatly affected by what is going on above us. It is essential to understand the weather structure, to know how the upper atmosphere relates to the surface, if a forecast is going to be accurate. 'Even without a weather fax, this knowledge will help you puzzle out the message in the sky, barometer and sea state', as it says in *The Mariner's Weather Handbook*.

In the same way, to think of children's behaviour only as 'good or bad', 'appropriate or inappropriate', and therefore only as something to be controlled, is to think of it in two dimensions. This ignores what might be going on above or below – 'the sky, barometer and sea state' – and therefore influencing the child. (And it is interesting how often a child can be 'a barometer' of a family's emotional wellbeing.) Parents and child are placed at right-angles to each other. By adding the third dimension, thinking about the child's behaviour as a communication, the hope is that this book will provide some understanding, in the moments when the obvious may have become obscured, or when supportive relatives and friends are not available.

A Sound Parental Instinct?

Donald Winnicott, the eminent paediatrician and child psychoanalyst in the 1950s and 1960s, talked of adults as having 'a sound parental instinct'. What a perplexing suggestion that is! What we call our instincts are often a combination of inclinations, experiments and things we have learned from our own parents. Bringing up a child is a complicated business – a bit of an experiment. This book does not present a plan on how to raise a child, but rather gives things to try which might work. The suggestion is that, given time and space to think, most parents can identify with a 'sound instinct' that tells them what to do, i.e. an instant way to respond to their children's behaviour. The problem arises when there may be a mismatch between that 'sound instinct' and the needs of a particular child. Then a parent may begin to feel hopeless, to flounder, to feel they have no 'sound instinct' about parenting – and a strong feeling that 'the books don't work'!

A truculent 11-year-old, Jack was brought to see me by his harassed parents who, during the first session, produced a verbal 'shopping list' of Jack's difficult behaviours. In analysing this list, we identified that most heat was generated around Jack's refusal to go to bed at a set time. His parents had been more than accommodating and reasonable in negotiating various bedtimes with him, but inevitably, each time a new bedtime was negotiated, Jack would produce a new fuss when the appointed time arrived. In our meeting the parents and I thought about the importance of Jack having a set bedtime. They quoted children's needs for adequate rest and sleep, and the fact that if Jack was allowed to stay up he would be difficult to get up for school in the morning.

Maybe children are quite capable of taking what rest and sleep they need and the demand for a regular bedtime is perhaps more parent-need-based than child-need-based! It may be a good enough reason for having a set bedtime but in this case it was self-defeating. Eventually, with great reluctance, the parents agreed to a new regime whereby Jack would be allowed to stay up as late as he liked – although after 8.30pm he had to be in a different room from his parents! – on the condition that he was down for breakfast at 7.30am. It was pointed out to him firmly that should he arrive for breakfast even at 7.31 any morning, then that evening he would have to go to bed at a time chosen by his parents. It was argued that an inability to get up in the morning would be a communication from Jack that he hadn't had enough sleep and therefore needed an earlier bed-time. For the first three nights Jack stayed up well past his abilities but always managed to be down for breakfast at 7.30am. Over the next few days he settled into a regular bed-time, coincidentally not much wide of the mark his parents would have set. On the eighth or ninth day he arrived for breakfast at 7.33 and his parents pointed out gently that he would have to go bed at 8.30 that evening, to which he retorted 'sod digital clocks!'

By freeing themselves from a 'cultural myth' Jack's parents were able to remove the battle from one area of his management. As this element of their relationship with Jack began to diminish, they were able to think creatively about how to handle other difficulties of his early adolescence.

So Donald Winnicott promotes the thought, 'What is the sound instinct of a parent and where does it come from?'

Knowing and Not Knowing

'You're 25, you think you know all about life, but, my God, this is something different...'

Father of a ten-day-old baby

'I was terrified, I heard her crying and I thought "I'm destined to answer that cry for the rest of my life". I was terrified...'

Mother describing the moments after the birth of her first baby

How and where does one learn to be a parent? Where do 'sound instincts of parents' come from? There is a prevalent idea that men and women will automatically know how to be a parent. As Jack's parents illustrate, our culture abounds with myths about what is 'good for children' and, like all myths, these myths about child-rearing are founded on reality. Children do need sufficient rest, but that does not mean that all children need the same rest! Child-rearing myths may reinforce the idea that parenting is a skill that can be taught, like training for a job or learning the rules of a game. Most people have a personal view of what is 'good for children'. Advice passed on (whether requested or not!) from grandparents to parents, from friends to friends, from professionals to parents, may reinforce the idea that there is only one right way of parenting.

'Being Good with Kids'

A little girl awoke on the morning of her fourth birthday party. She was excitedly asking which of her relatives would be attending that afternoon. Having greeted all the names with pleasure she said of one particular aunt, 'Good, I'm glad she's coming, 'cos do you know what, she's good with kids.'

This little girl was perhaps not only repeating adult conversations, she was verbalising something that we all know, that some people are almost instinctively 'good with kids'. It can be argued that this instinctive knowing what children require of one and being able to establish a rapport with a child may have little to do with knowledge about, or being an expert on, children. It is likely that we have all come across people highly trained in knowledge of children who find it very difficult to establish an easy rapport with them. So what is it that makes people 'good with children'?

A very deprived six-year-old from an inner city area fell hopelessly in love with her student teacher. One day the class teacher asked her why she loved the student so much. 'Because she's so clean' said the little girl. I find this comment absorbing. What was the 6-year-old trying to describe about someone who was clearly 'good with children'? One understanding of such a comment from such a deprived little girl could be that in some way the teacher represented the 'dream person' that she would like to become in later life, if you like a role model, an alter ego, some part of herself that she felt present, but unrecognised, by other people in her current predicament. *The Oxford Dictionary* throws more light on the discussion. It tells us that one of the origins of the word 'clean' is the German word 'kleine', meaning small. For meanings it gives: 'pure; free from foreign matter. Free from dirt or filth. Free from spiritual or moral pollution. Free from ceremonial or sanitary defilement. Clear of obstructions, inequalities or unevenness.'

So was this little girl picking up something of the qualities necessary to be able to be close to children? Is it something about being able to be small (i.e. vulnerable), being able to remain honest and to have a sense of equalness in one's attitude to children and evenness in one's handling of them? It certainly seems less a question of information about children and more to do with an indefinable 'something else'. This thought took me back to the question I raised earlier about you, the reader's, expectations of this book – are you expecting to have more information about children, or are you expecting to have more faith in your ability to parent... or what?

On Being the Expert

I remember very clearly that many years ago I was sent for extended teaching practice into a classroom run by a much older, experienced and indeed expert teacher. I remember how part of me despised her for her lack of knowledge of trendy methods, and how another part envied and respected her instinctive 'knowingness' about teaching. Beneath my desperate efforts to convert her to more modern methods, and despite my unswerving beliefs in those methods, I knew that, somewhere, she knew best. Under the umbrella of her knowledge I was able to experiment with thoughts and ideas about children, which she was not free to have – as she held responsibility for the children in the class. Looking back, it is interesting to remember the different relationship we each had with the class. Not surprisingly, the children seemed to have a much more relaxed and free relationship with me, it would not be unfair to say that at times they seemed more lively, spontaneous and creative in my presence. However, in times of need or stress they would quickly gravitate back to the security of the class teacher, knowing that she could be relied upon to be consistent and understanding.

In the same way, as a therapist I can only ever be 'a student' to the family. Literally in the last analysis, the child is the child of the parents. There is a sense in which the parents will always be 'expert teachers' knowing more than I.

What therapy offers people is choice, the choice to see and believe things in a different way, which may lead to an alternative way of behaving. As Adam Phillips has said 'therapy gives people an alternative life story'. So, a mother whose father left home when she was 7 and whose husband leaves home when her daughter is 7, may feel that the only message she can pass on to her daughter is that 'men are unreliable'. It is possible, however, that therapy would help her to explore and understand why these two events have happened in her life and enable her to offer her daughter a range of understanding about men. However, I have to respect that during and after their therapy parents may choose to parent in a very different way. So I have to be able to tolerate trying to persuade people what I believe, but acknowledge that they may not agree with me and may well continue in their own way.

So Where Do We Learn to Parent?

In the same way as I was a student in the classroom with the expert teacher, so children are students in the family. What boys and girls are studying in the family is how to be an adult, how to acquire adult skills, how to become a man, how to become a woman. We are all familiar with how small children will try to imitate their parents in order to be like them. I remember a 3-year-old trying to 'help' his father to clear an outside drain. Returning to his mother in the kitchen, he was clearly rather fraught and het up.

'Has daddy cleared it?'

'No,' replied the little boy, 'it's still blocked. Blast it!'

A 4-year-old boy was discovered by his mother sitting on his father's loo with a newspaper upside down on his lap, he fixed her with a steely gaze and said: 'Will you leave me in peace?'

In a family children are also learning how to be a parent. Most people will have some desire to do some things differently from the way their parents did it, equally many people are surprised to find themselves doing it in the same way. What our parents did is absorbed over a number of years, until it becomes an instinctive way of behaving. It is distressing for all parents, but particularly for parents where there is a real desire not to, when they find themselves making the same or similar mistakes as their parents. It is a sad truth of life that, emotionally, one cannot pass on what one has not experienced. A child may feel humiliated at the parents' attempts to 'do the right thing', be it a contrived or theoretical attempt at creative play on the sitting room floor or an anxious attendance at all school functions. The expectation is that we will be as good as parents as our own parents, if not better than them, but then that we will make the same mistakes.

If You Are a Single Parent

There is still a prevalent feeling that 'it is better to be a couple' if one is going to have a child. This has perhaps been more explicit in the past where there has been strong emphasis on the idea that it was essential for a child to have both parents living together. In this day and age we are beginning to think about the advantages and values of having one parent. Clearly, family structures are changing. There are lone parent families, adoptive families, same-sex parents, older parents, etc. (I am wondering as I write this book what kind of parents it will be useful for, and am hoping that I have found a philosophy appropriate for everyone.) It can be argued that in this fluid time for families, books on parenting are more important – and also more difficult to write – than they have ever been. There are now so many concepts of a family. However, it is potentially very comforting that there are so many ways and forms of parenting. There are so many people trying to make it work in so many different forms, races and cultures.

> 'A repertoire might be more useful than a conviction, especially if one keeps in mind that there are many kinds of good life'.
>
> *Adam Phillips*

A soft option?

Whilst I was putting the finishing touches to this introduction, I happened to see a snatch of a television programme on the pros and cons of smacking children. The audience discussion was dominated by a pro smacker who argued forcibly that 'children push boundaries' and a smack is often 'the only language they understand'. He saw any other form of discipline as a 'soft option' and the child 'turning you into the servant'. It was interesting in that calling a smack 'a language', this parent was able to construe adult behaviour as a communication. Children's behaviour, on the other hand, was simply divided into 'good' or 'bad' and had to be controlled accordingly.

What is a soft option in child-rearing? Certainly not understanding children's behaviour as a communication. Children need clear, firm boundaries throughout their childhood for several reasons. Boundaries not only help children to feel secure – this far and no further, mummy and daddy are keeping you safe by being in charge – boundaries also help children to develop a sense of self, as a unique individual, separate from other people. As the child develops a sense of privacy around themselves, and towards other people, they develop a respect for other people and for themselves. Of course children will 'push the boundaries' – that is how they learn exactly where a boundary lies. A smack will certainly show a child a boundary, i.e. how far they can go, but it may do little for developing mutual respect. In my experience smacking a child simply makes a child angry – and eventually that anger will be played out in one way or another.

Most children want to please their parents above all else. An eyeball to eyeball contact, a firm but kind voice repeating, 'What will please me now is if you will...' will show a child a boundary and foster respect and 'give-and-take' in relationships.

A good boundary is strong, but flexible. Boundaries help to keep us safe and help us not to behave in ways which may bring us sadness and regret. Boundaries are also there to be crossed when it is appropriate. If you are clear as an adult about your own boundaries and how to maintain them, then you will find it easy to give your child boundaries. Thinking about your child's behaviour as a communication, and trying to match your response, is no 'soft option'. You are communicating to your child that you understand how they feel, and that you can help them to find a better way of communicating how they feel. Your child is learning that by communicating their feelings in appropriate behaviour, they are not only respecting other people but also stand a much better chance of getting their needs met! It is hard work for you as a parent. It is very different from a 'soft option' where boundaries depend very much on the parent's mood in the moment. When tired, stressed, angry, unwell or even just feeling indulgent, many parents will admit to 'giving in' rather than maintaining a boundary. As an isolated incident in family life, this should cause no problem, but as a way of life for a child it can be disconcerting. The child who cannot rely on secure boundaries is likely to feel insecure and chaotic.

'For Now Sits Expectation in the Air'

It is no coincidence that a pregnant couple are described as 'expectant'. Parents are expectant in a number of ways. In the first chapter I want to discuss these expectations, beginning with what the baby isn't! Further chapters will go on to discuss specific ordinary problems of childhood, sibling rivalry, schooling difficulties, lying and stealing, bullying, how these behaviours may be understood as a communication, and when parents should begin to regard these behaviours as 'extraordinary' and perhaps seek professional help. In the final chapters we will reflect upon the impact of divorce on children and some of the ordinary and extraordinary problems facing mothers who work outside the home.

Children are born into a world of expectations, and parents and children spend the rest of their lives trying to extricate themselves from each other's inventions.

Great Expectations – How Children Change Our Lives

Y ou did not choose your parents. You took what you got and made the best of it. But the fact that you did not choose your parents probably did not prevent you from having a wide range of expectations from them as you grew up. When these expectations were met, they were the best parents in the world. When they were not met, it is possible you were reduced to anger, sadness, feeling you had drawn the short straw of the most insensitive and unreceptive parents ever.

At the same time, your parents will have been expressing their joys and disappointments about you. You will have learned very quickly how to please and how to anger them. Whilst your expectations of them may have seemed quite reasonable, you probably found their expectations of you at best unreasonable, and at worst controlling and crushing.

The Best Laid Plans

'Nobody tells you...nobody warns you what it will be like. We did talk about it, we did make plans...resolutions. We said we must make time for each other, we must share this and that, but no one prepares you for the...emotions. At antenatal classes it is all practical, changing nappies and the like...no one prepares you for the shock, for the feelings'.

New mother

It is difficult for anyone to prepare anyone else for the truth of having children. Perhaps in previous generations there was no preparation. People simply had babies and got on with it, doing very much as their parents had done. Nowadays, many couples think about and plan their lives with their future children. However, in these plans there is often an unconscious expectation that the baby will fit in with the plans. Whilst you are planning to adapt to your baby, there may be an assumption that the baby will also adapt to you.

'In the books it says do this and that, and the baby will do the other, but my baby hasn't read the book'.

So why did you want it, and what did you expect, when you took on this job of parenting – a 24-hour a day, seven-day a week job – for life – and seemingly without pay?

Pause for Thought

◆ Why did you want a child?

◆ Did you and your partner have the same or different reasons for wanting a child?

◆ When did you decide you would like a child, for example, when you first got together, when you decided to marry, a few years into your relationship?

◆ How influenced were you by family expectations that you would have a child?

◆ What were the three main expectations you each had of being a parent?

◆ Did you both have the same expectations, or different?

◆ Which part of childhood did you think you would most enjoy as a parent, eg a baby, toddler, teenager?

◆ How did you think a child would change your relationship with each other?

◆ How did you think a child would change your family and other social relationships?

◆ What did you expect to lose when you gained a baby?

Of course you may have had an innate urge to procreate, but that biological fact accepted what were the other concerns and reasons, thought about and not thought about, you experienced in deciding to have a child?

Social Expectations

'We couldn't conceive of not having a family'

Even in an age when couples are delaying decisions about

marriage and starting a family, in days of househusbands and of 'sharing the care', there seems to be a prevalent expectation that couples will have children. Couples choosing not to can be thought at best a little cold, and at worst selfish or unnatural. Although it may be a reducing tendency, a woman in particular who has not had children may be expected to express some sadness or sorrow at that fact.

'You will just die out' – continuing the line

> 'My parents thought he would be just like me. My father even said "there'll be another little George running about…"'
>
> 'My parents kept on about it… well, they didn't keep on about it but they just made us feel guilty… that we should be starting a family…'

A 4-year old, on hearing a relative had broken off an engagement, cried, 'But you will just die out! You've got to get married. You've got to have babies, or you'll just die out…'

Sometimes in families there may be a general assumption that the lineage must be continued, or else!

◆ This assumption may be very obvious, for example there may be a family business which it is hoped will be continued into the next generation.

◆ At other times it is much less obvious, perhaps being linked to a general human deep seated fear of 'dying out'. Is our mortality, and indeed our parents' mortality, made less painful if we have children to 'carry on' after us?

'Don't do it for us to have grandchildren' – on pleasing mum and dad

Pressure from grandparents for grandchildren can leave a couple feeling that they have only been an adequate or good-enough son or daughter if they have provided a continuation of the line. Sometimes parental pressure is overt, for example, 'I want to have my grandchildren whilst I'm young enough to enjoy them, when are you two going to get on with it?'

More complex is the message from the hopeful grandparent

who says 'Oh, don't have children for us, we've had ours, don't have them for us to have grandchildren'. This is a mixed message. In effect, such potential grandparents could be heard to be saying to their children, 'We have done something, and what does it mean that you haven't?' In saying 'don't have them for us to have grandchildren' they could be heard clearly stating to the couple that they not only want grandchildren, but they're missing something by not having any. By technically giving the couple permission not to have children, they are implying that it is something they should do!

Creative Fulfilment

Many couples can resist the pressures of older generations. Yet at some point in many relationships there comes a time when a couple will feel a desire to create something together, something good and 'ours' – i.e. creative fulfilment.

On the whole a healthy child validates feelings of virility, wholeness and well being in the parents. A healthy, thriving baby may be seen as an outward, visible symbol of a couple's creative and happy relationship. If you like, a neon-sign 'all is well here'.

> Childbirth is not only about a baby being born. Parents reproduce themselves when they bring a child into the world. This fact may be pleasing to some parents – and threatening to others. In times of stress parents may feel that a child has inherited 'the worst of both of us'.

Not just expecting a baby

- Do you remember how you felt in those first few weeks after you knew you had conceived?
- Did you feel a sense of pride, a sense of joy at the idea of your personal continuity?

During pregnancy parents may dream and talk endlessly of their hopes and expectations for their coming child. There may be the expectation of a perfect baby who will live out their hopes and dreams.

'I wanted a little girl, to dress her up, make her look pretty'

– such a wish takes little account of the fact that the expected little girl may turn out to be a tom-boy who will wear nothing but jeans and jerseys. The young couple who plan to return to the paternal grandparents' home in Yorkshire for the coming birth in case the baby is a boy, and therefore eligible to play cricket for the county, are taking little account of the fact that they may give birth to a male ballet dancer.

'If it's a boy...will he be a pig, will he be a chauvinist...' (expectant couple overheard in a restaurant).

Of course, during pregnancy you could only have unreal expectations of your child as there was no 'real' child on which to formulate expectations until the birth. When you first saw your baby you immediately modified many of your expectations. (A blatant example would be if you were convinced you were expecting a girl, and were then delivered of a boy.) But at an unconscious level it is likely that many of your hopes and expectations were still present.

I am always surprised in talking with other professionals about a child who is experiencing difficulties, when I hear the comment 'The parents have such unreal expectations.' I can only respond, 'Of course.'

> All parents have unreal expectations of their children. At some point all parents have to come to terms with the fantasy perfect baby and the reality of the one they have produced, an independent personality with their own desires, drives and ambitions.

Delight and disillusionment

A young mother who was enduring weeks and weeks and weeks of sleepless nights said, in a moment of poignant sadness, 'At the antenatal classes they had a doll; when they bathed it and changed it they laid it down and its eyes closed...I thought babies were like that.'

- ◆ How did you expect to feel during the first few months of parenting?
- ◆ What gave you the greatest pleasure, and what was most disappointing?

Mr and Mrs J. were describing how they expected to feel many things in the first few months of parenting, but they had not expected to feel disappointed 'Exhausted, yes, but not disappointed', said Mrs J. After the birth of the child, in amongst all the joy, some parents may experience a vague sense of disappointment. This may be obvious disappointment, like the baby not being the desired sex, but I am thinking much more of unconscious disappointment, that is, disappointment that people may not have thought about, or of which they may not even be aware.

Gains and losses

◆ What did you lose when you gained a baby?

It is highly likely that during your pregnancy many of your thoughts were focused on what was coming, what was to be, what was to be gained by having the baby. It is likely that you paid scant attention to what you might lose. I am interested that when asked this question, most parents seem to give the same answer:

'I lost her, and she lost her freedom' (new father about his partner)

The impact of a new baby on a couple's relationship can be tremendous. What Donald Winnicott calls your 'primary preoccupation' is likely to be the baby, not each other. You may both begin to experience a sense of disappointment at the loss of focus on each other. During pregnancy you were probably advised, and fully intended, to work hard to make time to be alone together as a couple after the baby's arrival. However, as one mother said, 'We wanted to be alone, we wanted to have time together, but no one prepared me for the overwhelming feelings for the baby that kick in after the birth...It was just very hard to think of leaving her even for a few hours.'

The First Task of Parenting – Childhood as a Time of Conflict

As a child grows there is inevitable conflict, in some families more than others, between the child growing into the kind of man or woman he or she wants to be, and growing into the man or woman that the parents may want him or her to be. As you begin to think less about your dreams and expectations, and more about the very real child that you have in front of you, you are beginning to negotiate one of the first stages of child-rearing. This first conflict may be seen as representative of all the stages of childhood, which are potentially conflictual. There may always be conflict between what the child wants to be and how you may want them to behave.

> Maybe parents do not survive childhood by solving the problems of childhood but more by tolerating the conflicts.

In a way, parenting is an act of faith. It is the child's responsibility to develop. He or she will learn to walk, talk, to read, to write, to socialise. It is the parents' job to have faith that this will happen in time, though it may be at a different rate to the boy next door, his girl cousin two years younger, etc.

You do not have to make your children grow up, you just have to provide the 'good enough conditions' for the child to thrive and make their way.

The key to providing 'good enough conditions' may be the ability to think about what the child's behaviour may be communicating and, most importantly, to whom.

Pause for thought

 ◆ What are the three most important things your parents gave you?
 ◆ How do they differ from the three most important things you would like to give your children?

Surviving the Experts

Did you notice how as soon as you became a parent you seemed to be surrounded by experts on parenting? Grandparents, child care books, television programmes, professionals such as health visitors and doctors, all help to make up a long list of people who seem to know best about your child. Other new mothers play their part. Whilst such friends, at times, may be of enormous support, they can also be subject to endless conversations of 'topping'.

> 'She had us up three nights last week'.
> 'Three nights! You're lucky. We haven't had a full night's sleep for ten days.'

Why can these 'experts' cause parents stress during those first early months? The answer has to lie partly in all parents' very natural desire to 'get it right'. It must also be linked with another expectation of parenting, that there is 'a right way' to parent, and that there are simple answers to childhood problems which can be applied to all children all of the time.

◆ Once parents feel free to think about their child's behaviour as a communication, then they have less need of 'experts'.

◆ Maybe the key to surviving parenthood is developing the ability to survive everyone else knowing what should be done, whilst you, as the parent of the child, remain fundamentally at sea!

◆ The feeling of being at sea may be an essential part of understanding your child.

> 'If we were getting it right, if we were good parents, we wouldn't have to come and see you'.

Feeling at sea, feeling you're getting it wrong as a parent, may be an indication that there is a living, growing, developing relationship between you and your child, rather than a kind of textbook, two-dimensional, 'child does this, parent does that' attitude. If you and your child are unafraid to surprise each other, then the relationship is alive and developing. I appreciate that the feeling of being at sea in managing a child can lead parents to feel helpless and that they have no 'sound parental instinct'. But in such times it may be useful to follow the advice given to me as a quite definitely below average student on a sailing course. I remember the skipper saying to me in a moment of exasperation, 'If you don't know what to do, put your rudder in the middle, and think.'

But where is the lifejacket?

Of course, it is while 'at sea' that parents most need each other's support, and single parents need the support of people around them. This period of surviving the experts may be compounded and made more difficult by another dream which may seem to be shattered.

A Baby Brings a Couple Closer Together

It is likely that during pregnancy you expected that the coming child would bring you closer together, would unite you into being a family. As a single parent you may have hoped that the coming baby would strengthen your bonds with your existing family. In the long run this may hopefully be true, but what raising a child also does is to highlight the differences between parents.

◆ When you came together to create a family you brought with you your own experiences of family life.

◆ Your histories may have much in common but they may also have much that is very different.

In raising your children you are forced, to some extent, to relive your own childhood. Memories will come flooding back to you as you bring up your children. For instance it is difficult to buy your child their first bicycle, without raising memories of receiving your bicycle, or not receiving it, whether such memories or happy or painful.

> Parenting will make you realise the different ideas you both have about parenting, and such potential conflicts between you have to be survived. The degree to which you can negotiate and transform conflicts will form the basis of your ability to handle conflicts over your children, and possibly with professionals, when your child enters the outside world.

A united front?

Some parents think that they must always be united, that they have to smooth differences over. It can be argued that the advantage of having two parents is that you get two points of view. Parents who feel they must present the same view may make children feel that there is only one right way to do things.

We learn to parent from our parents. Whilst it is likely that there may be common ground in these experiences, it is also likely that there will be huge differences. There may be much in your childhood that you felt your parents got right and you would want to do likewise with your own children. And you may swear that you intend to do some things very differently from the way your parents did. Whilst most people may swear that they intend to do things very differently from the way their parents did things, many often find themselves doing it in the same way! The natural instinct to do it the same way is so strong that it is almost impossible to ignore.

I was asked to see Paul, aged 9, because of his difficult and negative behaviour. During my conversations with the parents it emerged that the father's father had placed a heavy emphasis on good manners and appropriate social behaviour. The father was anxious to reassure me that, apart from demanding a reasonable standard, these were areas in which he did not pressurise Paul. Only the most outrageous breaches of etiquette were corrected.

In a family session, when I asked Paul what he felt his father most admired about him, he replied: 'When I do well at school'.

'Anything else?'

Silence. Paul shook his head. His father was surprised to realise that he was carrying on his own father's model of parenting, but in a different area. Paul was left as a child in the same way as he had been, feeling that he was only loved and accepted if he achieved in certain areas.

> Because you hold different views it does not mean that one of you is right and the other is wrong. It doesn't mean that one is a good person and the other is a bad person, it means no more nor less than that you have different views.

Ten-year-old Jimmy lived with his mother and step-father, regularly visiting his father who lived in America. His mother and step-father took a rather liberal and relaxed attitude towards Jimmy, believing that he would eventually find his own way in the world and that pressurising him into academic or indeed any other kind of success was not appropriate. His father, on the other hand, was very anxious that Jimmy should do as well as possible at school, and go on to university before perhaps following him into his business.

As Jimmy began to approach adolescence he found it increasingly difficult to cope with these two contrasting views. The matter was not helped by his parents' inability to respect each other's way of living. Jimmy's father would constantly criticise his mother for not being more rigorous about, for example, Jimmy completing his homework, and his mother would be critical of his father for placing so much pressure on him.

> What matters to children is the way in which you present your conflicts and differences, rather than the fact that you have conflicting views. 'I would let you, but daddy won't' may not be the most helpful approach.

The conflict became much more manageable for Jimmy when both parents were helped to present their differing approaches to life as alternatives of equal value, rather than an either or choice.

◆ A helpful way to present a difference of opinion may be something like: 'Mummy and I don't agree about this, but we have talked about it and on this occasion we're going to do things Mummy's way... it doesn't mean we will always do it Mummy's way, but that's what we've decided to do this time.'

What does being a family mean?

'We all have to do what everyone else wants... it's not fair. Nobody does what they want...' A 7-year old

'It's being snugly – I mean like watching *Star Trek*. My dad makes room on the floor cushions.' A 6-year old

Giving Them What I Never Had

Of course you want your children to have the things that you enjoyed and also the things that you never had, be they opportunities, possessions or leisure activities.

◆ How do you feel when your child does not seem to appreciate these things as much as you feel you would have appreciated them as a child?

Family life can be most disappointing for parents where there is an overriding desire that their children will live their unlived lives. By this I mean that children will follow the career, recreational activities, etc that the parent longed for as a child but was never able to have. This desire may be expressed with rather controlling views of how the child should be and should lead their life, even to the extent of a future career.

I remember talking with some very disappointed parents whose 11-year-old daughter had just failed to gain entrance into the school of their choice. She was about to begin school in a much less academic environment than the parents would have desired. It had long been their hope that their daughter would eventually take over the family business, and her lack of academic achievement was making this a less and less likely option. 'If she doesn't go into the business, she could do secretarial training or something, she needn't be a hairdresser.'

Me: 'She might want to be a hairdresser.'

Mother: 'She doesn't need to be...'

Me: 'She might want to be...'

Mother: 'Oh, my God!'

Recreational activities can be another source of disappointment. John may not inherit his parents' love of tennis, he may prefer to spend long hours playing computer games or skateboarding.

◆ Can your family tolerate such differences, differences of every kind, or is the philosophy 'sameness is togetherness' in following a set family pattern? There can be a fantasy that if everybody likes doing the same thing, then the family is closer than if they are free to follow their individual likes and dislikes.

Perhaps this is, in some sense, a legacy from images of the

family that were projected by the media in the fifties. The model was a family with mother and father having very distinct and different roles, the children modelling on the parent of the same sex, and always together. In some ways it may have been a true picture, perhaps families did spend more time together before the advent of such things as individual televisions in individual bedrooms. But it may have left a legacy that there is something wrong with a family that operates more independently.

A family where members have different interests, but take an active interest in each other's pursuits, can be just as close.

> Your expectation of what your family will be like will be coloured by your own experience of family life as a child. You are likely to have two levels of expectation: a conscious or thought-about level, the kind of family you planned to create, and an unconscious, not thought-about level, that is, the way your parents did it.

Doing It Better than Our Parents

'Help! I sound more and more like my dad.'

You are likely to be most distressed as a parent when you find yourself making the same or similar mistakes in child-rearing that you feel your parents made! This will be particularly disturbing if you have a real desire to be a different kind of parent. Perhaps a part of your not thought – about reason for having a child was to show your parents how to do it properly.

> It is a sad truth of life that, in the world of emotions, we cannot pass on what we have not experienced.

◆   If you experienced a loving and warm relationship with your parents, then you will instinctively pass this on to your children. If your relationship with your parents was less happy and constructive, then you may have to think more carefully about the way in which you parent your children.

For example, how did your parents handle your temper

tantrums? If your parents took the attitude that such behaviour warranted your being removed from the room, and left alone until you had 'calmed down' or 'were going to be reasonable' then it will be difficult for you to respond instinctively to your child's outbursts of behaviour in a different way and without the child feeling that it isn't contrived. Children are very quick to pick up when you are 'parenting from theory' and may feel humiliated at your attempts to 'do the right thing'.

'I was late collecting her. I was frantic, I kept thinking she'll be thinking I'm not coming. She'll be lost, the last to be collected. She'll feel so alone... When I got there she was fine, sitting on a chair looking at a book, she's different to me.'
(*Parent on a nursery school child*)

Follow your instincts

'I don't know how to be a father... not to a 10-year old... my father had left by then. What do fathers do with 10-year old boys?'

> It is difficult to give your children the good experiences you missed out on in childhood without raising the pain of the fact that you missed out. You may not want to remember that pain, or to think about it, and may try to block it out. It is difficult to block out one thought without unintentionally blocking out other thoughts.

When such occasions arise, you may find that you are not able to follow your own instincts, to do 'what comes naturally'. When I asked the above father what he would like to do with his 10-year old, he replied, 'teach him golf'. He had been unable to follow up this natural desire with his son, because it had evoked painful memories of watching the boy next door going off to play golf with his father, after his own father had left the family home.

Lazy hazy days of summer

The desire to do it differently from our parents may also be linked with another expectation in pregnancy: to keep in touch with our own childhood, an unconscious hope that maybe those idyllic times have really not passed – or that one day it'll be different.

> You will relive your own childhood through the experience of parenting, but you cannot change it. You can use the trials and tribulations of your own childhood as a key to understanding your child's behaviour. In this way, what was painful in the past may be positive in the present.

We are all familiar with the father who buys his son a train set with which the child never plays, but with which the father seems preoccupied. Likewise, the mother who encourages her daughter to have friends round to play, providing a delightful and welcoming atmosphere, cannot eradicate the experience of her own mother who refused or made it difficult for her to have such experiences. Of course it is essential to keep in touch with the child within, which also involves the ability to be spontaneous, to play freely in any given moment, to be vulnerable and to forgive readily – maybe this is the essence of all good parenting!

◆ When you are really struggling to understand your child, it may be helpful to reflect upon what you were like at the same age. What sort of child were you at the same age as your child is now? How was it for you? Such reflections may lead you to more understanding of, and wisdom about, your child than any book can offer. Thinking about yourself at the same age, what helped and what didn't, may be of crucial importance.

And What If You Are a Single Parent?

It will be obvious now that this chapter is written from the view of 'the ordinary couple' and this can be misleading. Whilst all children originate within a couple, you may be reading this as a single parent, either by choice or because of death or divorce. Support systems for lone parents are crucial. To some extent all that is written about the relationship between mother and father will be relevant to the lone parent and your support system. The friend, relative or childminder who shares the care of your child, and is seen to be openly supportive of you, may very well come into the kinds of conflicts with the child that I have written about as often occurring between parents.

Perhaps this book places emphasis on 'the couple', because there is still an expectation in society of a couple raising children. Now the expectations may not be so much that the parents are living together, but that they are both active in the upbringing of the child, both physically and emotionally. This perhaps raises another expectation relevant to the chapter.

◆ What are the couple's expectations of what the child will do for the couple?

It is very common in acrimonious divorce cases for aggression between the parents to be worked out over issues concerning the child, such as access or money. Such parents may often be very surprised when it is pointed out to them that they seem to have an expectation that they can use the child to carry on an unfinished argument or hostility between them.

It is equally very common to hear of a couple having a baby 'to save a relationship', be it a married couple or not. The expectation is that somehow having a child will cement the relationship, without the couple having to try to resolve their difficulties. Such a child may be a bitter disappointment to both parents if the relationship does then break up. The child too may feel they have a heavy burden to carry in life. I remember a 10-year old girl who was worrying both her teachers and parents with her general lack of confidence and feelings of failure. After several family sessions, she said: 'Well, I have failed, haven't I? I have failed!' What emerged was that unconsciously she realised she had been a marriage-saving baby and, aware of her parents' current unhappiness, felt she had failed in the purpose of her being.

A similar problem can arise when a mother decides to have a baby 'because I want a change', almost seeing motherhood as a change of career. If motherhood is disappointing, it is not easy to hand in one's notice!

Disappointment and Envy – The Problem of the Child-Free Couple

◆ The child-free couple may be a source of envy to parents, for whom in the hurly-burly of feeding, nappy changing and broken nights the joys of children may have temporarily been masked. I remember vividly one young mother expressing her hostility towards her children. When I reflected that she didn't seem able to enjoy children very much at the moment, she responded 'I'm too exhausted to enjoy them, I'm too exhausted not to enjoy them, I'm just exhausted...'

◆ Is there a sense that the child-free couple are seen to be living the unlived lives of couples with children? Their relative freedom to pursue their own interests, seemingly to come and go as they please, and relatively uncluttered homes may provoke the thought in parents that 'If we'd known what we were doing, we wouldn't have done it.'

◆ The child-free couple may provoke thoughts and anxieties about children that parents would prefer not to think, let alone express.

> Something we all know, but is very rarely talked about, is that most parents feel they hate their children at times.

A bitterly disappointed father, who found it very difficult to make a relationship with his daughter whose looks, personality and developing interests were a far extreme from what he would have hoped and wanted, burst into tears one day and said 'If I hadn't had her, I wouldn't want her, but I have got her so I love her.'

Another mother, describing how her very troubled 6-year old had lain down in a shop and had a massive temper tantrum, described her exhaustion and helplessness at coping with this very difficult child. 'I wanted to think, "Christ, I can't stand that bloody little monster any longer", but I didn't.'

'We Thought It Would Be Fun'

◆ Surely your greatest expectation in planning a baby was that it would be fun!

Your expectation was that the coming baby would be a source of joy, not only to you but to the outside world. When you are most worried about your children's behaviour, when things seem to have gone wrong or got into a muddle, don't ask yourself 'What have we done wrong?' or 'What is wrong with our child?' but rather, 'What is happening to prevent us all from enjoying each other?'

By now your expectations of me, the author, will have been met or not met. You may be both encouraged and disappointed with the book, as indeed one is in child-rearing. In the coming chapters I would like to discuss some of the ordinary problems of childhood, to highlight signals children may give to parents. I will also look at circumstances where these ordinary problems are no longer developmental stages, but have become 'extra-ordinary problems' in an attempt by the child to communicate an anxiety to the adult.

Summary

♦ Children are born into a world of expectations, and parents and children spend the rest of their lives trying to extricate themselves from each others' inventions.

♦ We learn to parent from our parents.

♦ Childhood is necessarily a time of conflict. Maybe parents do not survive by solving the problems of childhood, but more by tolerating the conflicts.

♦ It is normal to feel a sense of disappointment as well as elation after the birth of a baby.

♦ A baby may bring you closer together as a couple, but parenting will also highlight your different expectations of family life.

♦ 'Feeling at sea' about your child's behaviour may be an essential part of understanding that behaviour.

♦ Memories of your own childhood will come flooding back to you as you bring up your children. Being aware of this helps you be open to what your child is communicating, rather than being disappointed that she or he isn't following your script.

♦ Holding different views as parents does not mean that one of you is right and the other is wrong, or that one is a good person and the other is bad. It means no more, no less, than that you have different views. What matters to your child is not that you have conflicting views, but how you present those views to them.

◆ If sameness is always togetherness, can your family tolerate differences of every kind – personality, interests, expectations, etc?

◆ In parenting you cannot pass on emotionally what you have not experienced.

CHAPTER 2

The Stealing of Crowns – Sibling Rivalry

I t seemed a good idea at the time – to have more children! By the time you were pregnant for the second time, many of the expectations discussed in the first chapter will have been tried and tested. Now a further expectation comes into view – that your children will love each other and take a harmonious pleasure in each other's company. Whilst you were probably expecting the traditional sibling spats, you maybe did not anticipate the constant hostilities that frequently seem present as one child tries to make another's life a misery.

A Further Expectation – 'Someone to Play With'

'We didn't want him to be an only one, we wanted him to have someone to play with.'

'We were only children, if we died she'd have nobody.'

The most common reason given when I ask parents what made them decide to have a second child (usually out of my sense of awe at how they have managed the first) is that they wanted their children to be companions for each other. A small and wistful 7-year old once commented quietly in a family session when such a comment was made, 'But you didn't ask me if I wanted a sister to play with.' Would any child really choose to have a younger sibling?

'Their cousins play so nicely'

You may feel disappointed and dismayed that your children seem to fight and argue excessively. It is also likely that you worry 'what are we doing wrong?' – the fantasy being that this doesn't happen in other families. It is ironic in times of anxiety how one can suddenly be aware of exacerbating factors all around. A friend, recovering from major surgery, said he was surprised at the increase in the number of people in his home town in wheelchairs. Of course, the likelihood is that there was no such increase but that being in a wheelchair himself made him more aware of others in the same position. Equally, it seems that when parents are most worried and anxious about their own children's sibling rivalry, they feel surrounded by other families where total harmony seems to reign all the time.

Pause for thought

- ◆ Why did you decide to have a second or third child?
- ◆ Did you have different reasons for having different children?
- ◆ How did you explain to the existing children about the coming baby?
- ◆ Do you think they believed your explanation?
- ◆ How did your parents deal with your sibling rivalry?

False Expectations – 'It's Me You're Angry With...'

> The idea that siblings should get on may be that of the parents rather than the child.

It is rather like having a dinner party, where you invite a group of people who don't know each other but have things in common, in the hope that they will 'get on'. Sometimes they do, sometimes they don't. There is no guarantee, because other factors than having common interests and a friendship with you come into play – so it is in families.

It is never wise to ask existing children if you should add to the family. Firstly, it is an almost impossible question for the child to answer and, secondly, what do you do if they say no? Your first child is used to your sole attention and, if still a toddler, may have a sense that they rule the world. And why not? Their every need is met, usually, on request, leading them to believe that they are in charge of you, rather than vice versa.

> Remember, sibling rivalry is first and foremost a grievance against you, the parents, for having another baby.

When a rivalrous child is attacking their sibling it may be helpful to say something like 'It's me you're angry with for having Tom, not Tom.'

Is Sibling Rivalry Inevitable?

No, but it is a natural phenomenon.

The balance of relationships within a family will change with exits and entrances. Dr Penelope Leach describes vividly how the only way an adult can understand what it is like for a child to have a sibling is for you, the mother or father, to think of your spouse coming home and saying, 'Darling, you're such a wonderful spouse, I'm going to get another just like you, and she/he is going to come and live with us.'

If parents are sensitive to the feelings of existing children, and respond with understanding, rivalry may be kept to a minimum. On the other hand, it may not!

'We did everything right. We talked to him about the baby, we let him feel her kicking inside, etc...the baby bought him a present, we have gone on giving him special time...but he is so jealous'. (Desperate parents of a 5-year old)

It can be argued that the older the child when a sibling arrives, the less likelihood there is of intense sibling rivalry. The older child is likely to have established their identity and own life, and is, therefore, less threatened by the new arrival. Teenagers will certainly be more focused on their life outside the home. But as with other human predicaments, there are no guarantees.

'Why can't I have the money, you give Tom money.'

'Tom is only 4 years old.' (Angry exchange between 19-year-old son and father)

> Maybe what matters is not whether or not your children are rivalrous of each other, but your ability to acknowledge such rivalry as an ordinary problem of childhood. Helping your child to negotiate rivalry is as ordinary a task as helping him or her to learn to walk.

'He stole my crown, he stole my crown'

Eight-year-old Sam explodes and sums up the dismay he felt as a three year old on the arrival of his younger brother. He not only had to share the attention of his adoring parents and grandparents but. in his view, was usurped by him as the king of the family kingdom.

> For a child under 5, the arrival of a new baby in the family can raise a worrying question. 'Why did mummy and daddy want another baby, when they'd already got one?'

Tim's answer ...

Tim was 6 years old when his parents sought my help about his demanding and worrying behaviour. He was difficult to settle at night, never wanting to go to bed, and once he'd been put to bed, calling or coming downstairs at regular intervals. He rarely slept a full night, and would frequently wander into his parent's room demanding entrance to their bed during the night. During the day he was always 'on the go', constantly restless, both at home and at school. His parents described how, even if he was watching TV, he would be jerking and wriggling next to them on the settee. He frequently had minor and relatively superficial accidents, such as falling off his dining room chair, for which he would seek an inordinate amount of attention. He would sob, wail and demand endless cuddles and reassurance, even when his parents were sure that the accident couldn't have 'hurt'. Much of this behaviour had begun during his mother's pregnancy with the second child, and had been exacerbated from his sister's birth onwards.

...he was forgotten

I asked Tim's parents how his restlessness made them feel. They were frank in their irritation with him – 'it's impossible to even watch TV when he's around, he's always in the way...he's always on our minds.'

Children have very limited ways of telling adults when they have a problem. If they haven't the language then they are likely to fall back on behaviour as a way of communicating.

The problem for adults is that the child often chooses behaviour that does not accurately illustrate their problem – and then the behaviour itself is perceived as difficult and inappropriate. In Tim's case, his restless behaviour was construed as a problem in the family. But maybe for Tim, this problem was actually a solution. Maybe Tim felt he had to work very hard to stay in his parents' minds.

In a family session Tim said he thought his parents had got the baby 'in the night, when I wasn't there.' Tim seemed to fear that his parents had got another baby because they'd forgotten they'd already got one. He was worried he had somehow fallen out of his parents' minds, and could do so again if he did not constantly remind them he was around.

Tim's parents understand...

> Babies communicate by projecting feelings – the baby makes the adult feel what he is feeling.

Once Tim's parents were able to think of his behaviour as a communication, they found it much easier to manage. His reluctance to go to bed and disrupted nights were understood as his fear of leaving his parents alone together. He knew that if he left them alone they might make another baby!

> From a child's point of view, 'the problem' behaviour may not be a problem but a solution to a real worry or puzzle.

...and helped Tim to understand

◆ Tim needed to be helped to talk about his fears and anxieties. He seemed relieved when his parents gave him open and honest explanations about why they had had another baby. He was reassured that he had not been, and could not be, forgotten by them. His parents explained that although at times they might be thinking about other people and things, they both had a 'space in their minds' labelled 'Tim', and that space was always there, and so they could never forget him.

◆ Tim's behaviour could be understood as communicating

that he felt that babies got the better deal in the family. His parents began to think about what was in it for Tim to be the elder child in the family. What rewards did he get for being the elder? They realised that whereas it may have been appropriate to treat a 3-year-old and a 5-year-old in approximately the same way as regards bedtimes etc, now that Tim was 8 years old he needed some privileges for being the elder.

◆ Rewards, such as being able to stay up a little later, pocket money etc, helped him to establish his own particular place and identity within the family. Tim's destructive behaviour began to decrease.

◆ A slow build up to bed time enabled him to go to bed without too much protest. About 45 minutes before bedtime his parents would say 'Tim, soon it will be time for bed, what do you need to do before you go to bed?' Twenty minutes later they would remind him that he had 20 minutes more and a similar reminder was given at ten minutes. ('Ten minutes *more*' always seems longer and has a more positive connotation than 'Ten minutes *left*.'

◆ If he did wake during the night, his parents would reassure him that he was not forgotten, and return him to his own bed. Tim became generally more relaxed and less frenetic, his anxieties had been communicated and heard.

Sophie's solution...

Five-year-old Sophie had provided herself with quite a different explanation to the same perplexing question. Sophie was a naughty little girl. Any opportunity to disobey, make mischief, or spoil a family event or outing with a massive temper tantrum in public, was taken. Any attempt at disciplining her was met with massive sulks and an outburst of 'I know you don't love me.' Her parents were at their wits' end when they came to see me.

Sophie had a younger brother, born when she was nearly 3 years old. Her parents remembered with bewilderment that in the couple of months before her brother's birth, Sophie had frequently asked her parents, 'Am I a good girl? Am I a good girl?'

... *There was something wrong with her*

Sophie's mother talked at length of her deliberate naughtiness – 'It's as though she wants to be told off.' Maybe Sophie did, maybe she felt she'd done something wrong, or there was something wrong with her, and that's why her parents had had another baby. When children are persistently and deliberately naughty, it can sometimes be their way of trying to find out what is wrong with them. The hope is that if they find out the 'big wrong' and are punished for it, then all will be well – and in Sophie's case, the baby would be returned from whence it came! Her mother remembered rather movingly an occasion when she had been trying to read Sophie a story, but was frequently interrupted by her baby brother crying. 'Mummy, can't we put the baby in a cupboard and just get him out when we want him?' Sophie asked.

Sophie's parents find a solution

What did Sophie need to help her regain her confidence in the fact that she was loved and lovable? How do you give a small child the message that she is loved simply because she is who she is?

Sophie needed to be spoiled, i.e:

◆ To have special time and treats with her parents.
◆ To be surprised by them with sudden hugs or inexpensive little gifts or treats for no reason – not because it was her birthday, or she'd been 'a good girl', or achieved something, but simply because she lived.
◆ To have her parents verbalise that they enjoyed her company. It can be very helpful to such a child for parents to say 'I am enjoying this playing this game (shopping, driving to school, etc) with you' as an event is happening. In this way Sophie is reassured of her parents' pleasure in her.

The Importance of Spoiling

It can be a daunting task for parents to try to spoil a child who seems to be behaving inappropriately. Won't it encourage the child to persist with unacceptable behaviour?

There is a difference between indulging and spoiling. Allowing a child to be in control is a terrifying experience for the child. Children need and want the adults to be in charge. Giving a child special time and attention, in however small a way when she is troubled, can give the message 'We love you because you are you, even when you are being this version of yourself we find difficult.'

> 'Things are much improved, spoiling her really seems to be helping... but I'm running out of money.'
>
> *(Father of 9-year-old)*

Spoiling doesn't necessarily mean the giving of material gifts. Whilst these may be useful at times, parents are usually resourceful in finding ways of spoiling a child without breaking the bank!

Such spoiling should go hand in hand with firm, but kind, discipline. It may be acceptable to be jealous of your brother, it is not acceptable to communicate this by hitting him.

Loving and Hating

Seven-year-old David was referred to me because of his difficulty in making friends. I was assured by his parents of his close and loving relationship with his 5-year old sister, whom he was said to adore. His parents wondered if his closeness with his sister was preventing him from making friends, was it that he simply didn't need other children? They recounted how he was recently invited to spend the night at a friend's house. He had become highly distressed at bedtime as to whether his sister, Rowena, 'was all right' declaring he was missing Rowena so much that he wanted to go home. Indeed, he could not be persuaded to stay. I was also told of his terror of 'monsters and things that go bump in the night', often having nightmares that a monster had come into the bedroom to hurt him.

Magic thinking

At some point many children will wish their siblings dead, or at least that they will go away. It is also quite ordinary for children to wish their parents dead, or at least exiled for a while. Accepted as a normal human phenomenon, this should cause no problem. But sometimes such a wish, and the fear that it may come true, can overwhelm a small child.

David protects Rowena

For children there can be a real confusion between wishing something would happen, and making it happen, a sense of magical thinking akin to the adult experience of not wanting to say something out loud for fear of making it true. Why could David not relax and enjoy the company of his friends, whom he knew very well, without being so anxious about his sister's wellbeing? Perhaps his closeness to his sister was a communication of how much he'd wished she'd go away. His desire that something would happen to her had so overwhelmed him that he felt she was only safe if he was around to protect her. Separated from him, he was afraid that his wishes to harm, would harm her.

Inside and outside monsters

Children can easily be overwhelmed by strong, powerful feelings and need to find a way of communicating this to adults. David tried to describe 'the monster bit of himself' that wished to hurt his sister, and possibly his parents for having her, by his fear of the monsters entering his bedroom to cause him harm. He may have had at least two reasons for doing so.

◆ David could make sense of his overwhelming feelings by describing them as monsters.
◆ By personalising his feelings he was able to put them outside himself, i.e. it wasn't him who felt aggressive and destructive, but the monsters in the bedroom.

Terrified – or big and bossy?

David reacted to his fears of magic thinking by trying to protect his sister with a pseudo-devotion and care. Other children may react by becoming dominant and controlling, trying very hard to communicate that they are big, strong and powerful, in an attempt to master their destructive thoughts. In reality, they are often communicating how helpless and powerless they feel in the face of their own aggression.

A rather pompous, self-opinionated adult client had always maintained he had a close relationship and a deep affection for a brother born when he was 8 years old. I was suspicious. One day he told me how he remembered the baby being brought home and his mother saying 'This is your baby brother, and you love him very much.' We came to understand how he had spent his life trying to feel what his mother had told him he felt, but at the same time developing his superior manner in an attempt to dominate his aggression towards, and his rivalry with, his baby brother.

David's parents understand...

David needed:

◆ Permission to feel angry and jealous. He doesn't have to like his sister, he does have to respect her.

◆ David's parents talked to him about 'magic thinking'. Nothing bad is going to happen to his sister because he wants to hurt her. There is only magic in fairy tales.

◆ David needed to understand that his 'monster feelings' were ordinary. The family as a whole shared angry 'monster' feelings. Everyone talked about what made them very angry, and how they felt when they were angry. Again, it was stressed to David that 'monsters' only exist in fairy tales. But perhaps sometimes he felt like a monster and that was frightening – like a monster coming into his bedroom.

James thinks he'll banish the problem

'I remember when I was 4, sitting in the sandpit on a sunny day and thinking "isn't this happy" – and Stephanie got born – everything was all right until Stephanie got born...'

A pale, tense, 10-year-old James was trying to 'explain my life to you.' Clearly a bright child, he had always found it difficult to settle at his boarding school, making few close friends. He had initially made good academic progress but, over the three terms prior to his referral, his grades had consistently declined. He had been a weekly boarder since the age of 8 and had become increasingly reluctant to return to school on Monday mornings. His parents explained it had never been their plan for him to board, but from the age of 7 he had pleaded to do so and they had eventually reluctantly agreed. He persuaded them he missed being with his friends, and that he would love 'sleeping in dorms', and at boarding school 'you can play sport in the evening.'

'He really hates his sister, he makes her life a misery'

James' parents were worried and bewildered. Concerned as they were about his unhappiness, and lack of success at school, 'top of our list of worries is the way he bullies his sister.' I heard how he had always had difficulty accepting her arrival and over the years he had constantly hit, teased, bullied and provoked her.

Well, how would you have dealt with James?

James' parents were at their wits' end – 'We've run the gamut of our list of what to do, we've tried understanding, we've tried punishing, nothing seems to make any difference.' James' mother was particularly upset, explaining 'I frequently lose it with him, and give him a kick up the pants. I can't stand the way he treats her.' She confessed she often looked forward to his return to school on Mondays – 'life is so much more peaceful without him.'

If Your Child asks to Go to Boarding School

Why did James want to board? Was it, as he said, that he 'missed being with his friends' and that he would love 'sleeping in dorms', and at boarding school 'you can play sport in the evenings' – all conscious or thought-about reasons for James. Or was there another unconscious, or not thought-about reason?

Fighting like cats and dogs and the best of friends

> If problems hunt in pairs then so do feelings. For adults and children alike, loving and hating are always present together.

There is much truth in the old joke 'she's my best friend, and I hate her.' It is likely that your children are ambivalent about each other. You will have observed how they can fight like cats and dogs one minute and be the best of friends the next. A child like James, who wishes to harm his sibling enough to send her away, invariably gets into an enormous muddle for at least two reasons.

◆ Children are as good as lovers as they are haters. James had genuine feelings of affection for his sister. He wanted to hurt her, but he also didn't want to hurt her.

◆ Like most children, James' aggression was overwhelming for him and he feared that if he did harm his sister, then he would lose his parents' love. He found himself in a 'no win situation' when he hit his sister – it was a hollow triumph.

'Of course you can't board'

Perhaps James' parents gave him the wrong answer. Maybe James was setting them a test. He wanted to protect them and his sister from his aggression. He felt that the only way to do this was to send himself away from the family. He feared that maybe the same thought had crossed his parents' minds. So he asks 'Can I board?', hoping his parents will say 'Oh, no, of course not, we love you far too much, we'd miss you far too much, we couldn't even think of you being away at boarding school.' When he was allowed to board it confirmed his worst fears that he was not wanted within the family because 'I hit my sister.'

'And Then She Gloats' – the Importance of Triumph

Jonathan was 5 years old when I overheard him whispering to his 3-year-old brother early one morning, 'Billy, when you were asleep last night, I got up and had ice cream with mummy and daddy.'

If you have a rivalrous elder child, it is likely that two aspects of their behaviour will irk you most.

◆ You will be angry when they hurt the younger, more vulnerable child.

◆ You will be angry when they gloat over their siblings.

You may well have tried hard to give them some special treat or privilege, in an attempt to alleviate the jealousy, only to have them rush off and immediately rub their sibling's nose in it.

> Sibling rivalry is a natural phenomenon. The balance of a family changes with exits and entrances. Maybe gloating needs to be kept in similar proportion. You may regard it as an unpleasant character trait, but is it not one of the rewards of being the older child, to triumph over the younger one?

'The little ones get more attention'

Your older children may find it helpful when feeling jealous of your attention to the younger ones if you help them to think about how different children of different ages need different kinds of attention. Help your eldest to think about exactly how the younger ones get more attention. Likely answers are, for example, help with dressing, washing, feeding. Agree with them, that is a lot of attention, but that is, for example, 2-year-old attention. Do they want 2-year-old attention, help with the same things, or do they want age appropriate, 6-year-old attention? Make a list with them of what would be special 6-six-year-old attention, for example staying up later, pocket money, special treats a 2-year-old can't do, etc. In this way an older child may gain a sense that they are as much in their parents' minds as the younger, more actively demanding ones.

The Family Baby – How do You Feel When You Make a Mess of It?

An 11-year-old was watching her 14-year-old sister try on a particularly becoming bikini. Her sensitive mother, noticing her envy, said to her, 'When you're 14, you can have a bikini like Amanda's.'

'No,' the younger girl replied, 'when I'm 14, I'll have that bikini, all I ever get is what Amanda's finished with.'

Ten-year-old Jane was exploding with rage as she recounted an argument with her 12-year-old brother, over who should sit where in the car. 'Tim said he should always sit in the front of the car because he's older than me. I said to him, "You're always going to be older than me, at that rate I'm never going to sit in the front".'

One of your tasks as a parent is to help your child to come to terms with their incompetencies. To small children, the skills and abilities of adults can seem almost magical. I remember a schoolfriend telling me how as a child she thought that grown-up life would be so easy because 'adults know and can do everything.' It is hard to feel incompetent. At best, most adults have an ambivalent attitude towards their own incompetence, at worst it can make them feel angry and frustrated. It is sometimes difficult to remember that making mistakes is an important part of learning.

When does a Yorkshire pudding become a profiterole?

Can we relate to the young mother who, when having her in-laws to Sunday lunch for the first time, forgot to bake the Yorkshire puddings? 'Oh, I didn't worry,' she said, 'I served them up as profiteroles for tea!'

> How we feel about our incompetence may depend on how it is described.

Is a child shy, or do they have their own particular way of getting to know people?

Is the excited 4-year-old who rushes at arriving visitors, flailling at them with his fists, rude and aggressive, or just unsure of an appropriate way to say hello and show his great delight in seeing them?

No wonder our incompetence makes us angry; it reminds us all the time that we are not omnipotent, we cannot do and know everything.

'It's not fair, Paul can stay up late' – the oldest get everything

It is likely that your youngest child is not only envious of your skills but also those of their older brothers and sisters. Just as older siblings may misconstrue age-appropriate attention given to the family baby as a demonstration of favoured affection, so younger children may perceive the skills and privileges of an older sibling as favouritism. The younger child may feel that everything they wanted to do, the older one has done first, and set the family standard.

But don't pretend the older children are not more skilled...

Faced with the younger child's explosions at the advantages of the older one, their cries of 'it's not fair' and their very obvious distress and rage, you may have fallen into something of a muddle in handling the children. It is not uncommon for parents to describe handling a younger sibling's envy by keeping the privileges or advantages of the older child a secret or by allowing the younger child to do the same as the older child, for example, merging bedtimes, in an attempt to blur the differences. Such solutions can, on the whole, only lead to resentment and confusion.

◆ The older child may feel rightly robbed of the privileges and rewards of being the older child and also of the ability already discussed, to triumph over their younger sibling.

◆ The younger child may be led to a sense of hollow victory – they may have won the right to go to bed at the same time as the older child, but their envy of the older child's skills will remain.

> Pretending children are the same age, or have the same skills and abilities, will not make them the same age, and will not give them the same skills and abilities.

Helping the family baby with rivalry

◆ Verbalise the disappointment. Tell the family baby that you understand how disappointing it is for them to have to wait to grow up, but also highlight with the child all the exciting things they are able to do while waiting to grow up. They need to know that you understand their frustration and disappointment.

◆ Reward them for being the youngest in the family. This may involve making a double effort to ensure that they do not always wear hand-me-down clothing, etc, even if such clothing appears to be virtually brand new.

◆ Explain to your child how you felt about your own position in your family as a child. This can be useful both if your position marries up with the position of the child having difficulties or not. Just hearing how mummy and daddy felt when they were the same age can bring enormous relief to a worried child. A little boy, riddled with jealousy of his older brother's ability to go and play football for the school on Saturdays, took enormous pleasure in his father's story of how, when he was small, he used to hide his older brother's football boots just as he was going out to play in a match.

Do You Provoke Jealousy – Whether You Mean to or Not?

'Can you do magic?' asked Sam.

'It sounds as though you'd like to do magic,' I replied.

'Yes, I'd turn the blues into pinks,' said Sam.

Sam was the eldest of three children, having two much praised and adored younger sisters. From the time he was 7, his parents grew more and more anxious as Sam took every opportunity to 'dress up in chiffon and scarves', and generally pursue what, at the time, might have been described as 'girlish activities'. Anxiety about his sexuality was running high when his parents finally came to see me when he was 11 years old.

Do girls have a better deal than boys in the family and vice versa?

Sam was acting out an extreme version of a common envy that children experience, that is, to be the opposite sex. Sam had construed his parents', particularly his father's, delight in his younger sisters as being due to their sex. He feared he was somehow 'the wrong sex'. Sam was trying to be like his sisters because he thought that that would bring him closer to his parents.

'I can never get it right'

There will be times when you will feel as exasperated with your children's sibling rivalry as the mother who said, 'If I bring home two Kit-Kats, and let Penny choose before her brother, she'll say she chose the worst one.' But your child may also feel he can't get it right. We could understand Penny feeling she couldn't get it right, because what she wants is what her brother has got, a different sex.

Will they grow out of it?

> Sibling rivalry is rarely completely negotiated and the confusion and fears surrounding it are seen in adult life.

Most people have had the experience at work or socially, of having inexplicably strong hostile or confused feelings towards another person, which they do not understand and find difficult to manage. An adult client found it impossible to tolerate her landlady, often adding to her list of complaints, 'and that ginger hair!' One day she realised how the landlady reminded her of her powerful, ginger-haired older sister, in whose care she was often left as a child.

An ordinary condition

Envy and rivalry seem to be natural facts of the human condition. Adults come across it frequently in their workplace, and it is therefore not surprising that it is an issue children are likely to find in their 'workplace' – the home. If you can foster an attitude that love, affection and attention are not a cake, from which a slice is taken for one child, therefore leaving less to be shared between the others, but more like sun which shines and makes us feel warm, regardless of how many other people are sitting on the beach, then your children's sibling rivalry may stay in perspective. However, both parents and professionals will agree, that either we have to believe that some children are born more envious than others, or that at the moment we do not properly understand children with the most severe difficulties around sibling rivalry.

It's okay to hate your brother

> Accept that your children may not like each other. In so far as you can, foster an atmosphere of mutual respect rather than affection. Problems are most likely to arise if you make your children feel guilty or naughty for having ambivalent feelings about their siblings.

Perhaps the issue has never been summed up better than by the 8-year old, who described meeting her baby sister in the hospital, 'I ran over to the crib intending that I would love her all my life, but I when I looked in the crib, I was jealous.'

Can the Only Child have Sibling Rivalry?

Martha feels left out

Let us not forget the only child. Such a child may be considered to be free from sibling rivalry, but not necessarily so. I was once asked to see a little girl of 7 who was extremely irritating to her teachers. She was the sort of little girl who always seemed to be asking for unnecessary additional help. One teacher quoted a particularly irritating habit of, when writing in her exercise book, on reaching of the bottom of the page, she would go and ask the teacher 'Shall I turn over?' The teachers were sympathetic towards her, in a way understanding that her behaviour could be a communication that she needed attention, but somehow 'needing attention' had taken on a rather moralistic tone and was being construed as a fault, rather than a genuine need.

When mummy and daddy have fun at work and play

What emerged was that Martha was the only child, born ten years into her parents' marriage. Both parents had busy careers involving not only long hours, but also a good deal of social entertaining. Martha grew up feeling jealous of her parents' relationship, they were always going out together, to her it felt that they would rather have each other than her. They took a greater pleasure in each other's company than in hers.

Martha's solution

Martha's 'attention seeking' behaviour with the teachers was understood as her trying to work out 'am I wanted and accepted by the adults?' The problem was, her behaviour was so irritating to her teachers that she ran the risk of being given the very answer she so feared. Martha's behaviour left her feeling that whilst her teachers might remember her, they maybe didn't like her very much.

What does 'attention seeking behaviour' mean?

'Oh, she's just trying to get attention.'

You have probably used the phrase many times about your own children. Adding the word 'just' tends to give the impression that children should not try to get attention. The implication is that there is something wrong or greedy about trying to get attention for yourself. Attention seeking behaviour so often indicates that a child is trying to get attached, i.e. close to someone. Martha wanted to feel closer to her parents, she wanted them to enjoy having her around. She had misconstrued their absences as preferring not to be with her.

How the adults helped Martha

- ◆ Once Martha's teachers understood her need to be close, they found her behaviour much less irritating.
- ◆ They were able to help Martha to feel close in positive ways, such as sitting her at the front of the class and giving her special responsibility in the classroom.
- ◆ Martha's parents made a particular effort to have some special family treats with her each week and to tell her how much they enjoyed having her around. However...
- ◆ There are times, as you know, when parents do want to enjoy being alone together. Martha's parents sometimes had to explain to her that 'Mummy and daddy are having time alone together now. It's disappointing for you, but some day you will have a boyfriend/husband to go out to dinner with and to sleep with.'

Summary

◆ For adults and children alike, loving and hating are always present together. It is your expectation that your children will get on, not theirs.

◆ Small children may wonder on the arrival of a new baby, 'Why did mummy and daddy want a baby, when they'd already got one?' Was there something wrong with the first one, or did the first one do something wrong?

◆ Most children are ambivalent about their siblings. Whatever position a child has in the family, they need to feel that there are rewards for being in that place.

◆ Don't try to blur differences between your children, allow for both triumph and disappointment.

◆ Only children may feel jealous of their parents' relationship.

◆ Sometimes parents can, without thinking, provoke jealousy.

It can be argued that lying is an everyday part of life.

Goldilocks and the Little Don Quixotes – Lying and Stealing

'How can she do it, how can she look me in the eye and lie?'

(Parent of 10-year-old)

'Why does he do it? He knows it is so easy to check, he knows he will be found out, it's so obvious, why does he do it?'

(Parent of a 7-year-old)

'I felt stupid, when the others said what they'd got...(for Christmas)...so I said like we'd be going to Disney. I knew it was a lie, but then everyone was listening...'

(10-year-old)

'There's something wrong (with our relationship)...I mean...why can't she tell me, if she trusted me she'd tell the truth.'

(Parent of 8-year-old, sadly)

'Only Adults Can Do It'

Anger, hurt, puzzlement, feeling let down...lying and stealing seem to be perhaps the most difficult behaviours for parents to experience as a communication. When a child is found to be lying, it is not unusual for parents to report that the punishment was given not for the crime – but for lying. Parents can be equally horrified when they find a child is stealing, particularly when there is apparently no material deprivation within the family, or when the child is stealing relatively worthless objects.

Many adults feel lying is never acceptable, such behaviour is seen as being detrimental to an overall search in life for truth and goodness. At the same time many people will admit to 'white lying', lies where the intention is not so much to deceive but to protect another from pain. The thought is that no real harm is done by their telling, for instance making up an excuse not to accept an invitation. Others will admit to telling the truth with a slant on it. For example:

'Do you like my dress?'

'No, quite honestly'

becomes

'Do you like my dress?'

'Pink really suits you.'

As one mother said, 'How am I supposed to tell them off for lying, when they hear me lying on the phone when turning down invitations?' Equally, many people will admit to trying to create a false impression in many parts of their lives. It may be living in a particular house or driving a car beyond their income. It may be exaggerating the size and importance of a job.

Pause for thought

◆ How are you lying at the moment?

Living a Lie

◆ It can be argued that lying is part of life.

◆ There is a sense in which adults make things up all the time, whether it be to impress, to dress down, to emphasise a point or detract from a point!

We now have politicians admitting in public that they were 'economical with the truth'. In this sense lying is shifting the focus, 'putting a gloss' on one aspect and hiding another. It is a way of living, be it in daily conversation or in other areas such as clothes, make-up, housing.

◆ Sometimes we have to lie in order to tell the truth. What looks like lying may in fact be a way of making the truth palatable.

◆ Many people will despise others found to have been 'living a lie'. Is this because part of being human is living with the fear of being 'discovered' in some way? Perhaps this is one of the reasons adults find it so difficult when children lie, perhaps it resonates with a real human fear – the fear of 'being found out'.

Pause for Thought

- ◆ When did you lie as a child?
- ◆ Can you remember why you lied, and how you were feeling at the time?
- ◆ How did your parents react to your lying?
- ◆ How did you feel about what they did?
- ◆ How do you feel when your child lies? What does it make you fear about a) your child, b) you as a parent?

Are All Lies the Same?

Children's lies tend to be less divided into white or other lies. 'A lie is a lie' is often the parents' line. But just as adults deceive in different ways so do children, and different lies, at different ages, can be communicating very different messages.

Lies typical of children

- ◆ Lying over trivial matters.
- ◆ Boasting lies – lying about experiences and achievements.
- ◆ Lies that explain how I feel.
- ◆ Disassociated lies.

Lying over Trivial Matters – a Developmental Stage

> 'Did you clean your teeth?'
> 'Yes'
> But the toothbrush is dry and the cap of the toothpaste is not thrown into the hand basin as usual!

You are more likely to be irritated than worried by lying over trivial matters. You are probably infuriated at the futility of such lies, 'She knows she'll be found out, it's obvious, it's so easy to check on and yet she goes on doing it.'

- ◆ Trivial lying is usually at its height between the ages of 4 and 7 years.
- ◆ At this time, such lying can be understood as a developmental stage for the child.

Until such an age your child perceived you as knowing all

about them and their world, almost magically being able to sense and meet their needs before they voiced them. This gave them a tremendous sense of security. However, part of your child's quest for independence is to begin to desire a secret life away from you.

◆ This quest for independence may be communicated by your child lying to you. 'If I lie to mummy and daddy, and do not get found out, then maybe mummy and daddy do not know everything.' Your child may construe this as proof that they have a private life, and that they can now be independent.

◆ They are beginning to experience exerting their own wishes against yours successfully.

Jamie (aged 7) was expected to perform various tasks, such as making his bed before he went to school in the morning. Frequently when he was ready to leave for school his mother would ask him if he had made his bed and he would say 'yes'. As soon as he had left the house, Jamie's mother would discover that in fact the bed was unmade. Punishment seemed to bring about no improvement. Jamie's mother decided that as Jamie didn't make his bed he would have to sleep in it unmade. He, paradoxically, began to make his bed of his own volition, albeit sometimes when he came home from school rather than before he went!

Now we are 7

If your child continues to tell excessive trivial lies after the age of 7, it is likely that the lying is less a stage of development and more a communication.

◆ Is your child telling you that they have not quite completed this stage of growing up?

◆ Are they telling you that they feel intruded on by you?

◆ Is it possible that they feel you know too much about them?

◆ How much age-appropriate freedom do they have?

◆ Are there some areas where you should be 'letting go' now the child is 7? For example, if they don't make their bed, they sleep in it unmade rather than you enforcing the rule.

Boasting Lies – Lying about Experiences and Achievements

Jean's party

Jean, aged 9, had caused a rumpus at school by inviting several children to her birthday party. The invitations were given verbally and Jean's description of the conjurer, etc who was to attend caused much excitement. When no written invitation appeared, most parents telephoned her mother to verify the event. However, two girls turned up on the Sunday and of course there was no party organised! Jean's parents were horrified, why would she lie in such a way? A party for her birthday had not even been discussed.

Further exploration revealed Jean to be a child seen by other children as something of an 'oddball', an outsider, who was rarely invited to other children's parties. What emerged was a picture of a little girl with very poor self-esteem. She was hurt and bewildered by her unpopularity, and sought to 'buy' friendship with good things to offer such as her party. For a few days it seemed to work, she was the centre of attention with her description of the event to come. For a while she felt 'good enough', liked and valued by her peers.

Colin's presents

Colin, aged 8, would often boast about his lavish Christmas and birthday presents. Other children would gasp with envy as he described his exciting latest holiday adventures, etc, etc. In reality the presents didn't exist and the holiday, if it happened, was much more ordinary than Colin described. However, he felt he could gain popularity by causing envy. Somewhere inside he did not feel 'good enough' to be loved and admired for himself. He had to 'put a gloss' on his personality.

Daisy's test results

Daisy's parents had a terrible shock at the latest school parents' evening. Aged 11, Daisy had been reporting excellent test results to her parents, telling them that she had finally been placed second in her class.

The reality was that Daisy's performance was more or less

average academically. She had sought to impress her parents with spectacular results in an attempt to gain their love, praise and recognition. She felt these were conditional on her good achievements, rather than freely available simply because *she is*!

◆ From birth, the two things children are most commonly praised for are their looks – 'what a beautiful baby' and their achievements – 'she was walking at 11 months ... talking by 18 months ... reading before she went to school', etc.

◆ Sometimes children come to believe that they can only be praised and loved for such progress. Such children live in a precarious world, putting themselves under extreme pressure to succeed for fear of losing love and approval.

When success is a burden

A very bright 10-year-old appeared for his session distressed and irritable following a school award ceremony, where he had carried off most of the class prizes. 'Now I've always got to do it,' he sobbed. 'I've always got to get an A in everything.' His success had begun to be a burden instead of a motivation. He saw a direct equation between the amount of his success and the amount his parents were able to love him. Failure academically meant failure to be loved. Once he had an A he always had to get an A.

Avoiding the muddle

It is not necessarily the case that such children may have only been praised for success. In a home where achievements are highly prized, a child may quickly make a muddle that achievements are all that matters, or what matters most, to the parents.

◆ How much do you think you only praise your child when they are following your script?

◆ How much do you surprise your child with rewards, emotional or material, for no obvious reason?

◆ How do you celebrate your child because they are who they are, and not for what they may or may not achieve?

'*I love you, I don't like your behaviour*'

Often parents will use this phrase to explain to a child that it's not the child they don't like – it is their behaviour. But from the child's point of view they are all the things that they do – it is hard for a child to distinguish between the two. The importance of acts of 'surprise spoiling' is that it communicates to the child that not all love has to be earned. They don't have to go on achieving in order to maintain their parents' love.

> On the whole, children want to please their parents. The problem arises when they feel they can only please their parents in a certain way by following a set script.

Tolerating our own incompetence

'To live a creative life we must lose our fear of being wrong.'
(*Joseph Chiltern Pearse*)

Children may find it very hard to come to terms with their own incompetence. Even older siblings, let alone adults, may be perceived as much more able in every area than they are. One sees this very clearly around the age of 2 or 3 when a child drops something or falls over and responds, 'I meant to, I wanted to...' even sometimes doing it again to prove a point!

◆ Your child may be envious of the skills and abilities of older people.
◆ This envy can lead to an impatience about growing up.

> Your child's envy and longing to grow up gives you an important task. You have to enable your child to tolerate being the age they have to be and help them to look forward to being older. You have to help them not to lose the fun and excitement of being the age they are – and not to regard 'now' merely as a time of waiting to be competent.

◆ Part of growing up is accepting that we cannot be good at everything and that there will be areas of incompetence.
◆ Children (and adults) will sometimes lie to cover up their incompetence (the classic must be the 3-year-old running into mummy crying, 'Mummy, some little girl wet my knickers!').

◆ A child may lie for fear of being abandoned or punished for being incompetent.

How parents can help

◆ Reassure your child that it is all right not to know, that even parents and teachers were once small and unknowing, and had to struggle to learn and master skills.
◆ Tell your child stories from your childhood that illustrate your struggles to come to terms with your incompetence.
◆ Tell your child stories of your incompetence as an adult! Explain how you feel about your incompetence.

> Your child may lie as a way of communicating that they fear rejection. But they are also communicating how they see you perceive your own incompetence.

◆ If your child is telling boasting lies, think about the culture around incompetence in the home. Is one sex allowed to be incompetent and not another, eg is it all right for mummy not to be able to reverse the car but appalling if daddy dents the number plate?
◆ Do you react to your own mistakes with, 'I was so stupid...I was really dumb...I felt such a fool...I didn't want to look a fool...I didn't like to say I didn't know' or by anger, 'How was I to know?...I should have been told!'
◆ Such responses may communicate to your child that there is something wrong with making a mistake. What your child needs is the idea that whilst one endeavours to do one's best in life, incompetence is part of being a human being.

Lies that Explain How I Feel

Ellie was 7 years old when she and I met. She had been causing concern to her teachers for some time but her referral to me had been precipitated by a rather dramatic incident in the classroom. One Monday morning she had arrived at school very distressed. She eventually told her teacher that over the weekend her hamster had died and that her mother had put it in the dustbin. She had been given the hamster for her birthday by her father shortly before he had left the family home.

The teacher took Ellie's distress seriously and at 'news time' the class had a little goodbye ceremony for the hamster. Ellie continued to be upset for several days, by which time the teacher raised the matter with her mother.

It emerged that Ellie did not have, and never had had, a hamster, let alone one recently deceased!

> Sometimes children will tell a story – a complete fantasy – as a way of explaining unhappiness or experiences they do not understand.

Ellie knew she was unhappy, she knew she felt bereft but she couldn't put her experience into words. She made up a story that made sense to her. It was an explanation of her feelings linked to an experience to which she could relate. So often adults will use metaphors to explain how they feel about an event, 'I felt as if I'd been run over by a steam roller.' Ellie was doing the same but because she was a child, she was omitting the words 'as if' – to her it felt as though this event had happened.

Avoid punishment

◆ It is important not to punish your child for telling lies to explain how they feel.

◆ Explain to your child that they are telling that it feels, for example, as if a beloved pet has died, and no one cared or understood their pain.

Disassociated Lies – It Wasn't Me!

Perhaps even more difficult for parents are 'disassociated lies'. Sometimes children under extreme stress, feeling very unhappy, will appear to cope very well with life. However, they can often be described as having one irritating and perplexing flaw. They will lie and maintain a lie, even after they have been found out. They have a gift for keeping up a plausible and a convincing lie under questioning. If they can be persuaded to admit to a lie they may apologise, but may very quickly commit the same offence and lie about it again. So what is such a child trying to communicate?

◆ Such a child believes he is telling the truth.

◆ You may well have had the experience of a small child with an imaginary friend, such as Christopher Robin's 'Binker'. Your child may have used the imaginary friend as a scapegoat for their own misdemeanours. In a similar way, under extreme stress, an older child may split off part of themselves, almost as though it is another person. The part that gets split off is likely to be the part that the child construes as 'the naughty part', the unlovable part of themselves.

◆ The idea in the child's mind is that if they disown the unlovable part of themselves, then their parents will only be aware of the lovable in them.

◆ Such a child, asked if they are lying, replies quite honestly, 'No', because they have separated off the person who did commit the offence.

◆ If you can persuade such a child to admit to their offence, understand that they are likely to be making an admission of guilt and not be understanding or accepting the consequences of their behaviour – any pain or distress that they may have caused.

◆ It is highly likely that they will do the same thing again.

The good guys v. the bad

Earlier in the chapter I talked about how the child who lies may have a sense that there is something 'wrong' with them, something unlovable that has to be redeemed and rectified if they are to maintain their parents' love and affection.

I was asked to see a girl of 12, Amy, who had attended the same school since she was 5. As she moved through the school, each class teacher had his suspicions that she was responsible for sporadic patches of fairly serious stealing. Each time Amy was questioned she would be co-operative, charming, open, and deny guilt, steadfastly looking the teacher in the eye. Nothing could be proved, and in any case, Amy seemed so plausible. The staff reasoned that it would be impossible for her not to show traces of anxiety in lying about such serious offences.

A few months before her referral to me, Amy had been

caught! She had initially denied the most recent spate, but when presented with the evidence admitted it and offered a direct apology, although her teachers had commented that they didn't believe she meant it.

Over the next few weeks, more evidence emerged implicating Amy with previous thefts. Amy was referred to me not for stealing, but because she seemed depressed. Indeed she was, for what Amy was beginning to realise was that it was indeed she who had been stealing. There were not two Amys, a bad one who stole, and a good one who didn't. Previously she had disassociated herself from the Amy who stole, and appeared plausible in her lying, because she actually believed she was telling the truth! At the time of her discovery her apology rang hollow, because although she was admitting her guilt she remained disassociated from the Amy who had caused so much pain and distress, and who was now to be punished.

Stealing

Where will it lead?

◆ You may be very frightened if your child is found stealing, particularly if it happens on a regular basis.
◆ You may be frightened about 'what have we done wrong' as parents.
◆ You are also likely to be frightened about your child's future – will they be a delinquent, a petty criminal, a train robber?

What does it mean?

'I needed something so I stole it.'
'What did you need?'
'Dunno, it's not the stuff...like I nicked...it's like inside.'
A 9-year-old struggles to explain his persistent stealing. His mother died when he was a baby. Although brought up by loving grandparents, he was left with a sense that he had had something and lost it. His stealing was understood as him trying to steal back his mother.
◆ Children steal because they feel they need something, emotional rather than physical, and that they haven't got it.
◆ Children steal because they feel they had something

important emotionally and have lost it and are trying to get it back.

◆ Such children will often steal completely worthless objects, bits of string, rubber bands, the odd piece of chalk, etc. Such a child is trying to tell you how they feel about themself. When a child loses something important emotionally, they are likely to blame themself for the loss. What did I do to lose the person I loved, or to lose the affection I once had? Am I not worthy of being loved? Am I a useless bit of string, rubber band, odd piece of chalk, etc...

◆ Remember, it is often quite difficult for children to articulate what they need except in physical terms.

> Most children steal on one or more occasion, be it a forbidden biscuit or sweet, or something larger, but continual or persistent stealing may be a desperate communication.

A sign of hope

Winnicott says that stealing can be understood as 'a sign of hope'. It can be argued that the greater the value of the things you steal, the more hope there is for you in the future. The child who steals is likely to have some hope that they deserve things, that they have a right to good things, love, affection, time, admiration. Such a child is fighting for their place in the world.

A similar child in the same position who doesn't steal could be understood as feeling worthless and has no rights on other people.

> As Bowlby says, a lot of delinquent behaviour comes down to people trying to get close to each other.

A Shocking Solution

◆ If your child is stealing, shower him or her with spontaneous affection, kindness and treats.

◆ By doing so you will give the message 'You are valuable, you are loveable, you are worthy, because you are you.

- Spoiling your child can be a way of saying 'At the moment you are a version of yourself that we love anyway, we love you whatever you are like.'
- Such a message indicates to a child that their behaviour is part of them, and that they are loved just the same.
- Set a firm boundary on your child's stealing. Explain to them that stealing isn't working for them. It isn't getting them what they need. Explain to them that they steal because they feel bad inside, but when found out stealing, they feel even worse about themself. Sometimes drawing a vicious circle can help, for example:

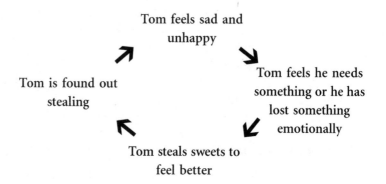

Tom feels sad and
unhappy

Tom is found out
stealing

Tom feels he needs
something or he has
lost something
emotionally

Tom steals sweets to
feel better

Who Has the Stealer Robbed?

I was recently asked to see a university student who was one of seven children. Her mother was a single parent and worked long hours to give the family a reasonable standard of living, often returning home mid-evening, understandably tired, and with further work to do. Stephanie described how difficult it was for any of the children, but particularly the older ones like her, to have any quality time or conversation with their mother. Weekends were a hurly-burly of housework and individual activities.

She recalled being taken as a child to the local fair by her mother. It was a bank holiday Monday. The other children were all occupied for various reasons. She described her pleasure in having her mother's undivided attention and then how, as they walked home, her clutching various trophies from the fairground stalls, she began to feel uneasy and unhappy. On arriving at the house, she hid her spoils in the bottom of a drawer.

◆ Stephanie felt that she, and perhaps her siblings, could only have quality time, affection, understanding, conversation with their mother, at the expense of siblings. She was left with a sense that all gratification was stealing. She had little sense of adults wanting to give to her spontaneously. As she walked home from her splendid afternoon at the fair, she felt like a criminal who had stolen something, not only from her deprived siblings, but also from her busy mother. She had robbed her mother of being at work.

Not surprisingly Stephanie was finding it very hard to enjoy successful relationships as a young woman. As soon as she became close to someone, she felt overwhelmed with guilt that she was stealing the relationship from someone else.

'Mummy Has It All' – Stealing Because I'm Envious

When your child was a baby all good things – food, comfort, etc – came from you. Part of growing up is realising that other people than mummy and daddy can give us good things. Ultimately, we learn, that we can satisfy our own needs. However, Melanie Klein has written about the muddle that can arise for some children who do not successfully negotiate this stage of development.

'All good things I have come from mummy.'

↓

'Mummy has all the good things in the world.
She possesses them.'

↓

'Therefore, I can only get good things from mummy.
I cannot own them myself.'

↓

'I am envious of mummy.'

↓

'I feel resentful.'

Envy and resentment

I have already talked of feelings hunting in pairs. The other side of envy is resentment. A resentful child will find it difficult to negotiate the necessary stages of being dependent on adults. Adults know it is difficult to feel close and trusting of someone they resent.

◆ Children afraid of being dependent may adopt an 'I care for nobody, no not I' attitude to relationships.

◆ They may show little concern for other people.

◆ They may lack respect for other people and their possessions.

◆ The bravado 'I care for nobody, no not I' may lead the child to stealing, i.e. simply taking what they want without asking for it.

◆ Such a child may be communicating real distress, a feeling of being deprived because others have so much.

◆ This is a serious muddle and if you feel this applies to your child, then seek professional help. Such a child may be communicating that they somehow feel abused by other people. The risk is that their stealing may lead to even more worrying abusive behaviour towards other people which will be discussed in the next chapter.

An Extraordinary Problem

Stealing may be regarded as an ordinary problem of childhood until it becomes compulsive. When a child feels unable not to steal, when they are locked into this way of behaving, then stealing becomes an extraordinary problem, requiring professional help. The communication has changed. Such a child is living as though they can only get what they want by stealing. They have lost the sense of listening and responsive adults who can meet their needs.

Summary

◆ Children who steal are not telling adults what they want, they are telling them how they feel inside.

◆ Most adults lie in some way or other in their lives.

◆ Maybe adults are so enraged by children's lying because we all live with an unconscious fear of being 'discovered' in some way.

◆ Lying over trivial matters may be a developmental stage for a child. Boasting lies may indicate that a child only feels valued for his or her achievements. Such lies may also indicate a child has anxieties about their own incompetence.

◆ How you feel about your incompetence in life will affect the way your child views his or her incompetencies. Part of growing up is accepting that we cannot be good at everything and that there will be areas of incompetence.

◆ Sometimes children will make up a fantasy story to explain an unhappiness or a worry that they cannot put into words.

◆ Children steal because they feel they need something emotionally which they feel they have not got. They may also feel they have had something important emotionally which they have now lost.

◆ Stealing can be understood as 'a sign of hope'. The child who steals may be fighting for their place in the world.

◆ It is difficult for children to distinguish their behaviour from themselves. If you tell your child 'I like you, but not your behaviour' they are likely to hear simply hear you saying 'I don't like you.' Children who lie and steal need to be reassured that they are loved even though they are being this difficult version of themselves.

◆ Avoid punishing children who lie and steal. Point out to them that lying and stealing simply isn't working for them. It is not getting them what they need. It is not making them feel better, indeed, it may be making them feel worse about themselves.

Bullying can be
understood as
an extreme form
of persuasion. CHAPTER 4

When Words Fail – Bullying

'I am rough and tough,' said 9-year-old Gemma, raising both arms in the air in a gesture both menacing and defiant.

'I am rough and tough.'

'You're rough and tough,' I affirmed.

'Yep,' another dramatic gesture, this time nearer my face.

'And if you weren't rough and tough, what would you be …?'

Tears sprang into Gemma's eyes, her cheeks flushed. 'Well,' she said, rubbing both her hands over her face. 'I used to like people, but nobody liked me, so now I'm rough and tough.'

'Do people like you rough and tough?'

'No, but I don't cry any more.'

Adults Bully

Whilst many childhood behaviours fall into disuse as we grow up, bullying seems to persist into our adult life. Society itself seems to have ambivalent reactions to it, sometimes applauding it.

'I slapped her into place.'

'I gave him such a hard time he eventually left.'

These may be sentiments sometimes admired in dealing with 'difficult personalities'. So why the paradox? Bullying goes against the basic human instinct to protect the weak and vulnerable but, paradoxically, the desire to bully seems to be a fundamental predicament of human nature.

Few parents can tolerate the idea of their child being a bully, even fewer can bear the thought of their child being bullied. Adults are often filled with a sense of dread, hopelessness and rage about bullying, be their child the victim or the bully. Perhaps these feelings are linked to our own relationship to the two key feelings at the heart of the bullying relationship – domination and fear.

> Can the reader honestly say they have never felt like bullying someone, even if they have never acted on that wish?

Pause for thought

- ◆ Do you remember bullying anyone as a child? How did it feel?
- ◆ Did you ever watch someone else being bullied? How did you feel?
- ◆ Were you bullied as a child? Why? Who did you tell?
- ◆ Have you been bullied as an adult, for example in the workplace, in a relationship? Did it feel different to being bullied as a child? If so, how?
- ◆ Have you been bullied in the last 12 months? How did it feel at the time?
- ◆ What is the difference between persuasion, charming, coercing, manipulating and bullying?

An Ordinary Problem

A 10-year-old boy was referred to me because of his constant bullying of his 7-year-old brother. Paul had never seemed to accept the arrival of Ian and took every opportunity to make his life a misery. He was also almost consistently rude and aggressive to his parents, having frequent dramatic outbursts of temper. The family had struggled for several years with this behaviour, but sought my help as the school was now reporting complaints of Paul bullying other children.

In our first family meeting Paul presented as an articulate child with a mature vocabulary. I noticed that whenever he made a point to his parents, he would do so emphatically. When they disagreed, paused to respond, or if Paul just felt he hadn't been heard and taken seriously in the general melée of conversation, he would reiterate his point more firmly. On some occasions he would stamp his feet, bang his fists and almost cry. When I asked what was making him so angry he said 'No one listens to me, I'm not important', and began to weep uncontrollably.

> Bullying can be understood as an extreme form of persuasion.

Paul began to bully at the moment he felt hopeless, hopeless about being heard. We began to think of his problem not as 'no one listens to me', but that he felt bullied by his parents producing his sibling. He felt they had never heard his overwhelming sense of being usurped by his brother. His life had become an attempt to bully his parents into understanding how he felt.

He felt helpless and vulnerable in the face of both his parents' power – and outrageous behaviour. He tried to overcome these feelings by being a strong and powerful bully. The vulnerable and frightened Paul had become the vicious, powerful Paul. Again a circle drawing was helpful to Paul.

**When Mummy and Daddy had another baby...
Paul felt left out**

Mummy and Daddy 'are cross

Paul felt Mummy and Daddy didn't understand

Paul bullies Mummy and Daddy to listen – Paul feels big and strong

Paul felt frightened, hopeless and angry

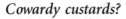

Cowardy custards?

We are all familiar with the idea of bullies as being basically cowards. What may be less obvious is a bully's vulnerability and pain. Paul had 'an ordinary problem of childhood', he felt unheard. He resorted to inappropriate behaviour to try to get heard. He ended up feeling even more alienated. When he was bullying – the active one – Paul felt stronger and less vulnerable than when he was being bullied – the passive one.

'I Wanted Him to Feel as Bad as Me – Passing on the Pain

◆ Children who are bullies have often been victims in some ways themselves.

◆ The child who feels afraid and anxious may look for another child to carry that feeling for them.

◆ The bully/victim relationship is a passionate one. The bully and the victim are connected to each other – they are the two sides of the same coin. We can think of bullying as a friendship that can't find a way of making itself work. It can be an inappropriate way of trying to become closer to someone. Be in no doubt, the bully wants to be the friend of the victim. It has similarities with 18-month-to-2-year-old toddlers who often think the appropriate way to approach another toddler is to push them over.

◆ Some children may feel so bad about themselves that they feel they deserve to be punished. They may unconsciously seek this punishment from a bully at school.

Kevin was 7 when his father finally left home for good. Until then the father was frequently missing for weeks at a time and Kevin's mother had long since chosen not to question him about his absences rather than risk 'a God almighty row'. Following the separation Kevin had frequently been let down on visiting days, waiting excitedly for his father, who never turned up.

During that year he changed from being a rather quiet and submissive child to being a rather sadistic and vicious bully, picking on his victims for no apparent reason. After a particularly vicious attack he was asked what he'd gained by making his victim so unhappy.

'Cos I feel bad... he's bad now,' replied Kevin.

Kevin wanted his victim to feel as bad as he felt. He was articulating the power/domination relationship at the heart of bullying. He felt afraid, alone, isolated. He sought a way of getting rid of that pain, the pain of feeling ignored. He thought that by making another child feel the same, he would feel better. Of course, for a while he did, he felt powerful, but it was a hollow victory. As his fear returned, he became hungry for more victims.

Parent Bashing

Such children do not just choose other children as their victims. Parents, teachers, swimming coach, etc can all come under fire. 'Parent bashing' is a remarkably common phenomenon (as indeed is 'granny bashing'). You will be familiar with the child who has a difficult day at school and 'takes it out' on you at the end of the day. Your sympathetic enquiry about how the day has gone is likely to elicit a torrent of abuse and complaints about you.

Children who are bullied often find themselves behaving out of character. Generally, they may behave quite confidently, but find themselves unable to do anything but cower in the presence of the bully. Unfortunately, cowering increases the bully's sense of power. It is important as a parent not to cringe and cower but to withstand your child's bullying attacks and try to make sense of their behaviour for them.

Simon was a very bright 8-year-old. His father was a successful property dealer who was having a difficult time during a slump in the housing market. When Simon was trying to bully his father, he would often shout something like: 'It's no wonder you can't sell houses anymore...' His father found it very difficult not to take such comments personally and to feel hurt and bewildered. 'It's not that I can't sell houses, it's that the general market has slumped' he reported to me sadly in a meeting. His was finding it difficult to deal with Simon's bullying behaviour because, like all children, Simon knew his Achilles heel.

When your bullying child turns you into a bully

Ten-year-old Margaret had made a repeated attempt to bully me into sitting in a small, child-sized chair in the room whilst she sat on my 'teacher's chair'. Eventually she advanced towards me with a pair of scissors pointed at my eyes.

'Do be careful, you might hurt someone with those scissors,' I said.

She pushed the scissors closer towards my eyes. This was the finale of an escalating number of threatened attacks on me, which were typical of her behaviour towards her mother and other children.

'I'm frightened you might hurt my eyes with the scissors. But I know you do not really want to go on bullying people. So I am not going to let you bully me by changing my seat, I said to her.

For a few seconds there was an eyeball to eyeball confrontation before she relaxed and said with a mixture of petulance and defiance, 'Well, send me back to class then', ie, another invitation for me to bully her. I reiterated that I did not wish to be a bully, and perhaps we could think about what made her feel so angry and helpless. At this point, Margaret burst into tears and our work was able to reach a successful conclusion.

By challenging me to send her back to her class Margaret was also inviting me to be firm with her, to set clear boundaries for her. However, the manner in which she said it could have made me respond with an angry, bullying: 'Well, yes, get back to your class.'

> It can be a fine line for you as a parent to distinguish in the heat of the moment between being firm, but kind, and bullying your child.

'You will enjoy it or else'

A friend tells an amusing story from his childhood. He and his brothers had wanted to make a tent in the garden. For quite a while they struggled with an old sheet and some bamboo sticks. In desperation they called upon their mother to help. She too struggled with the task, and eventually went into the house to find some more appropriate props. Whilst she was gone, the children drifted off to play. After half an hour of struggling, the mother managed to erect a satisfactory tent. She informed the children:

'It's safe to play in that tent now.'

'Oh, we're not playing that anymore,' replied the children.

In a fit of frustration their mother declared, 'You'll get up that garden and play in that tent and enjoy it – or else.'

In ordinary family life a lot of bullying goes on but it is not called bullying. Children bully parents, and parents bully children. Parents often call their bullying discipline and control. Children's bullying may be regarded as constant demands, nagging and defiant behaviour. Parents can seem and feel enormously powerful to children as they are growing up. One of the tasks of childhood is to find solutions to the power of the parent and some children may think that bullying the parent into submitting to their wills is an appropriate solution!

So what do discipline and control, nagging and defiance have in common?

> The common task of both parents and children in a family is to try to be heard properly, to feel recognised, to feel present and to have their needs recognised, if not always met.

Both parents and children will realise that there is a lot of frustration intrinsically built into this process, and as there is no such thing as a perfect parent (or indeed a perfect child!) bullying is almost bound to happen. Some family members may feel that it is necessary to insist other people do things, to force on other people what they want. Others will not.

> What differentiates a forceful person from a bullying person is the way in which the other person responds. The parent, or indeed the child, who stands firm against a bullying demand, prevents the other person from becoming a bully. So we can think of bullying as a relationship between a forceful demand and an appropriate response.

Defiance is Important

Children aged between 3 and 8 years old will try very hard to bend their parents' will to theirs. If you always do what your child wants then you, of necessity, make your child into a bully. It is important that you meet the demands of your children that you want to, that you think are appropriate, and stand firm, but kind, over other demands.

> It is easy to make a child into a bully by granting his or her
> every wish.

In early childhood, the child has a mission of trying to get
his or her needs met. If your child feels secure and confident
that you will hear their needs, and respond appropriately, they
are not as likely to have to fall back on bullying tactics as the
child who feels unheard.

Michael makes dad hit him

Twelve-year-old Michael was in his first few weeks at boarding
school. An only child, from an affluent background, he had
been used to little resistance to his demands from his parents.
He had always known that he would go to boarding school, but
when the time came he was filled with a sense of panic and
demanded that he should attend a more local day school.
Michael's father found himself up against the one demand that
he could not meet. There was a long family tradition of
attendance at a certain school and he was quite adamant that
Michael was going to keep up this tradition, mainly because he
honestly believed this was the best school for Michael to
attend.

Michael's first few weeks at school were miserable. Placed in
a dormitory with four other boys he found the lack of privacy
almost intolerable. Much more used to adults than peer group
company, he found it difficult to make friends in his new
environment. He became more and more distressed, phoning
home six or seven times a day. He demanded constantly that
his parents remove him from the school – a demand which the
parents continued to resist.

Over that first term, the parents worked hard with the
school staff to help Michael to settle. By the end of the first
term he did seem to be calmer and was phoning home less
often. However, during the penultimate week of the term,
Michael's father made a firm, but not over-the-top, correction
of Michael's table manners at Saturday lunch. Michael reacted
violently, throwing down his knife and fork and starting to walk
out of the room. His father ordered him to come back.
Michael refused. His father rose from the table and grabbed

Michael's arm to try to make him sit down again. Michael jerked away from his father, and swore at him. His father slapped his face.

The family were both distraught and puzzled by this totally untypical incident in the family. On returning to school Michael again became distressed and unhappy and eventually his housemaster sought my professional advice.

Michael explains his muddle

◆ Michael explained that although he had begun to comply with his parents' wishes for him to stay at this school, he believed that if they really knew how unhappy he was, they would let him go to a day school.

◆ Unconsciously, he provoked his father to strike him as a way of communicating to his father how awful he felt. It was as though he was saying to his father, 'Now can you hear me, now will you take me seriously?'

◆ Michael understood that his outburst at his father's correction of his table manners had nothing to do with what was happening at Saturday lunch! It had been an outburst of his deep-seated anger and resentment at his parents' refusal to comply with his wishes. He had experienced his parents as bullying him to stay at school.

◆ He had learned how to bully from his parents giving in daily to his demands, and had eventually bullied his father into striking him.

'There's nothing wrong, but things are in a muddle'

This family provides a vivid example of everyday miscommunications within families that can so easily lead to one or other member feeling that when words fail, bullying may be the only viable option.

It may be dramatic to suggest that had Michael had a less insightful housemaster, family relationships within Michael's family as he approached adolescence might have irretrievably broken down, but it is certainly a possibility. Instead, both Michael and his parents learned to find more appropriate ways of meeting each others' needs.

> Bullying should never be tolerated in a family or in a school. The parent or teacher who understands bullying as a communication and deals with it as such will not make the bully feel even more isolated, alienated and generally bad about themself. Such an adult is likely to provide a helpful and therapeutic bridge between home and school.

'My Mum's in a Bate', – Mirroring Family Relationships

Bullying has a number of faces. I have already referred to the fact that children who bully have often been victims themselves. This seems obvious where a child has directly suffered verbal or physical abuse. Less obvious is the impact on children of how the adults around them treat each other.

Discord and harmony – an uneasy balance

> Children's relationships with friends are likely to be a copy of how they see their parents' relationship.

Whenever parents complain to me about siblings fighting, one of my first lines of enquiry is how much fighting goes on between the parents. Children are astute observers of their parents' marriage. Sometimes children's behaviour can be a way of showing parents what they are doing to each other. Of course it is normal for there to be discord in parental relationships. What matters is the balance between discord and harmony. Children are constantly witnessing shifts in the balance of power between their parents, often demonstrated by their readiness to play parents off against each other, such as 'Dad, can I have my pocket money?' when mum has already said no.

◆ Children may be both intrigued by the way adults negotiate the balance of power in relationships – and puzzled by it.

◆ It is not so much the balance of discord and harmony in your relationship that matters. What matters is how it is presented to the children. Parents should communicate to children that in relationships the balance of power is fluid. The aim is not so much balance as fluidity. If one parent constantly moans about the power of the other parent, then the children are not going to understand this sense of fluidity in relationships.

Playing as a way of understanding

> Children also use behaviour to 'play out' situations that perplex them. By re-enacting seemingly unfathomable situations children can come to an understanding of them.

So in another sense bullying may be an ordinary problem of childhood. Children will experiment with both being in charge and being submissive.

A 12-year-old learns to be a man

There were many complaints about 12-year-old Matthew! Near the top of the list was his rude and aggressive behaviour towards his mother and also towards his female teachers. At our first meeting, the mother broke down and said: 'He's so rude, he's so aggressive...I just feel bullied by him.' I asked who else in the family might be considered a bully. A picture emerged of a caring and concerned father who found it difficult to express feelings of tenderness and kindness. So, for example, if the mother were ill, the father might express his concern for her by saying in an irritable and angry voice: 'Oh, go on, go to bed, I'll see to things here.'

Matthew was growing up with the notion that 'men bully women'. He was developing into an adolescent tough on women. His behaviour was being construed as bullying. Matthew was confused by this understanding of his behaviour. As far as he was concerned, he was practising how to be a man, not how to be a bully.

In a similar way a girl who consistently sees her mother bullied may grow up with the notion that women sacrifice their needs to men. In later life she may display behaviour that would give people the idea that she felt self-sacrifice was something wonderful and special. Nothing could be further from her thoughts, she is simply experimenting with being a woman.

Co-operation or Submission?

Marie's parents had separated when she was 9, but in the ensuing two years her parents had 'shared the care'. The parents lived within streets of each other and Marie and her sister spent half the week with each parent, still able to attend the same school. This arrangement seemed to be working well, partly because of the enormous amount of effort both parents put into it. They seemed to have managed to stay together as parents, if not as lovers. For this reason, when Marie was referred on account of her bullying, I was able to see the whole family together.

What emerged was a picture of a family very much dominated by the mother's controlling behaviour. What had seemed like co-operative management of the children emerged to be the father almost always bowing to the mother's wishes.

In her relationship with her peers, Marie was not only modelling on her mother. She was also acting out her deep-rooted fears and anxieties about her parents' relationship. To the outside world they seemed to have achieved a remarkable feat. In reality, the relationship was full of unspoken tensions and hostilities.

If Marie could not control her parents, she would certainly try to control everybody else.

Jennifer had a similar cause for bullying. At our first meeting Jennifer drew a picture of a face with terrifying teeth – 'It's a scary face,' she said, 'my mum's scary face.'

'Your mum has a scary face?'

'Sometimes. My mum's scary face is really scary. My mum's scary face takes out my soul.'

Family sessions revealed a mother desperately doing her best but who was unwittingly bullying her children. Her own mother had been a cold, authoritarian figure. She was determined to have a closer and warmer relationship with her own children, which she did. However, at times, under stress or acute anxiety 'to get it right', she would remain loyal to her own mother, and either lose her temper, or demand that the children share their troubles with her. Needless to say at such times they were reluctant to do so.

A muddle arose in the family of 'mum has a terrible temper'. At times the children were terrified of her, and the father was forever trying to smooth things over, but at the same time was desperately upset and helpless in the face of his wife's outbursts.

Mummy bullies for everybody

No wonder Jennifer was a bully. However, another thought emerged in family meetings. Was the mother carrying the 'bullying' for everyone else in the family? People were afraid of the mother's outbursts, but they were more afraid of their own anger and desire to control. As mummy was the angry bully, no one else had to be! Of course, as the muddle grew, so unconsciously the mother fell more and more into her role of bully. Father was helpless and frightened by his own anger, and so was unable to support mother in managing hers.

'This thing of darkness'

So how can it arise that parents can unwittingly bully their children? How can a parent not notice that they are bullying their own child?

In Shakespeare's *The Tempest*, there is a moment on the island when Prospero is asked of the monster Caliban,

'Is this yours?'

'This thing of darkness, I acknowledge mine' Prospero replies.

> You may bully your child when you perceive him as a replica of yourself, full of your 'thing of darkness'.

◆ It is hard to see in your child parts of yourself that you dislike and are trying very hard to change and transform.

◆ If you are trying to stamp out something in yourself, you are likely to want to stamp it out in your child as well. This can lead to rough and tough discipline, either physically, or in critical and sarcastic verbal bullying. Your child may then be left feeling guilty, and you are left feeling a sense of failure as a parent.

The Aggressive Victim

'*He lies down and shows the others his belly – of course they bully him.*'

Why are some children more bullied than others? Why do some children, as the teacher describes above, seem to invite bullying? 'Mind you, she asks for it', is so often the irritated last phrase in any adult's description of the frequently-bullied child.

Some children seem to seek to be an irritant to others. A highly irritated 11-year-old stomped into the kitchen where I was talking to his mother; the cries of his 8-year-old sister could be heard in the background. 'Mum,' he said, 'I'll kill her, you told me not to touch her, but I'll kill her.' As he sloped off, the mother turned to me, 'I share his feelings,' she said, raising her eyes heavenward as the grizzling 8-year-old entered the room, demonstrating how this particular child was regarded as 'agent provocateur' within the family.

> Donald Winnicott talks of the 'nuisance value of symptoms'. Children who invite bullying are making themselves a nuisance to somebody else and that may be a very important communication for them.

'I'm not a no one'

If mum and dad are shouting at you, then you know you have made an impact on them. As one 12-year-old said to me recently, 'When she (mum) is shouting, I know she knows I've got a life, I'm not a no one.'

Children who constantly try to get under other people's skin may be experiencing a real dread – perhaps all our true dread – of being unnoticed and ignored. This 12-year-old felt intensely isolated, and preferred the satisfaction of feeling that his mother hated him to the anxiety of not being sure whether she noticed him. Children and parents who get into this situation need some help in looking at more effective ways for the child to make an impact on the parent. It is remarkable how often when I ask parents, 'How would he know if he was making an impact on you?' the response will come back along the lines of, 'Well, when I shout, he jumps to it.' The irony is that when parents and children do get into a bully/victim relationship, it is often because they are trying, in totally inappropriate ways, to get closer to each other.

Bullying is contagious

It is interesting the way that one of the impacts of bullying is that it makes adults want to bully the child into behaving differently. There is a sense in which bullying is contagious. Your role as a parent is to stop the game of 'pass the parcel' and to avoid bullying the bullies. The importance of such bridges and parent/teacher communication will be discussed in the next chapter.

If Your Child is Being Bullied

- Encourage your child to talk about being bullied and not to feel ashamed of it. Reinforce to your child that it is not their fault they are being bullied.
- Show gentle and mild curiosity in your child's predicament. Ask him 'I wonder what it is about you that makes so and so want to bully you?' Without blaming, help your child to think about his part in the bully/victim relationship.
- It is the responsibility of adults to ensure no bullying takes place at either home or school. If your child reports bullying then tell a responsible adult as quickly as possible. Your child may initially protest, but will also be relieved that the adults are in charge.
- If your child is bullied, or becomes a bully, use this as an opportunity to think about how you, the parents, are getting on together.

Summary

- Bullying goes on all the time in most families but it is not called bullying.
- Bullying is an ordinary problem of childhood. It becomes extraordinary when a child feels bullying is the only way of being heard.
- Children who bully often feel bullied themselves.
- Bullying is one way children find to pass on emotional pain.
- Children can often invite parents to bully them. It is a fine line between being firm and kind in setting clear boundaries and bullying children into behaving in a different way.

When children
go to school,
parents go back
to school.

CHAPTER 5

'Honey and Bitter Aloes?' – Schooling Problems

'This is not altogether fool, My Lord'

(*Shakespeare*)

'Growing up is not all honey for the child, and for the mother it can be bitter aloes'

(*Winnicott*)

I have a vivid memory from my early days as a young teacher in charge of a reception class. On the Monday of the second week in the autumn term, I heard a loud altercation between 4½-year-old Peter, who had been in school a week, and his mother who was collecting him as usual at the end of the afternoon. On going to investigate I discovered a furious and scarlet Peter who was refusing point blank to sit in his pushchair. His mother looked bewildered, explaining how she usually had the greatest difficulty in getting him to walk!

First Encounter with the World

School is a child's first major encounter with the outside world, and whilst most children seem to take this step in their stride, it can prove a confusing and anxious time for parents, as Peter's mother soon discovered. The 4½-year-old toddler Peter, who had been more than happy to be pushed around the shops in August, quickly turned into an independent and stroppy schoolboy within a week in September.

Pause for thought

- ◆ Do you remember your first day at school?
- ◆ How were you prepared for school?
- ◆ What would have made your first days at school happier?
- ◆ What was your main anxiety when your child began school?

When your child started school you probably experienced natural anxieties about handing your child over to an unfamiliar adult's care. Will the teacher understand your child, will she be able to read his little signals in the same way as you do? Will she know this child is special, different from all other children, because he's yours? Will she protect him adequately, taking his upsets, and joys, seriously?

The answer to most of these questions is 'no'. The teacher will not have the same emotional bond, the same sensitivity to the child as the parents. That is not her job. Her role is to provide a warm and trusting environment in which the child is able to develop confidence and skills to explore the world and to also realise that good things can come from other people as well as from parents.

The class teacher is often the child's first significant contact with the outside world and he may experience the same love and hate for her, as he does for you, his parents. Whilst you may be delighted if your child settles well into school, it is also natural to feel at some times envy and rivalry towards this other adult who is seemingly as important, if not more important, than you for a significant number of hours a day.

'Miss James says, Miss James says...that's all we hear nowadays.' *(Parent of reception class child)*

Of course, you will feel anxious and disappointed if your child doesn't like their teacher. But you will feel outraged if the teacher doesn't seem to like your child.

'And I not knowing how I cried out then...cried it all again'

In Shakespeare's *The Tempest* Miranda describes to her father how she has told Ferdinand, her new found love, of her childhood experience of being cast away at sea, adding, 'and I not knowing how I cried out then, cried it all again.'

> Your attitude to your child's teacher and school will be
> influenced inevitably by your own school experiences.
> When your child starts school, you re-live starting school.
> The child goes to school, the parents go back to school.
> School is a potent symbol for adults and we cannot
> underestimate its resonance.

It is not unusual for a highly successful, articulate parent to
blanch at the suggestion that their child's difficulties in school
should be discussed directly with the headteacher. Many will
admit to feeling quite scared, 'The problem is, the headteacher
thinks she's talking to an adult, but inside I'm a quaking 6-year
old.'

> Your early school experiences may be indelible. What can
> be guaranteed is your worst experience will become your
> crusade at your child's school gates, for instance if you
> were bullied at school, then you will crusade against
> bullying at your child's school.

A group of mothers asked first to recount their main
anxiety about their child starting school, gave a predictably
wide range of answers, 'Will he cope with the demands?', 'Will
she have friends?', 'Will he be bullied?', etc, etc. When asked
then to recount one outstanding memory of their own school
days, all gave stories illustrating their experience of their main
worry for their child! This said, there are also universal
childhood problems around schooling which will now be
addressed. How you react to and manage these problems may
depend very much on your own childhood experiences. The
advantage is that your experiences will sensitise you to the
things your child might suffer from at school.

Failure to Settle in School

For most children the transition from home to school goes
relatively smoothly. There will be inevitable conflicts in moving
from one world to another. These may range from different
values, different expectations to a different routine. It may be
acceptable at home to take your lunch on a tray in front of the

television, this will not be acceptable at school. Alternatively, crisps may be emptied from the bag into a bowl at home, but may be eaten from the bag in the playground. On the whole, give or take the odd wet bed, the odd temper tantrum, the mild refusing to eat, the over-tiredness, for many children this transition will go smoothly.

Coping with like and unlike

Other children experience a real difficulty in settling. Of course much will depend on the similarity of the two worlds. It is not surprising when a 5-year-old Asian child, recently arrived in the country, experiences difficulty in starting school in a class where she speaks no English.

In this book we are very much thinking about children's behaviour as a communication, and the inherent difficulty of working out what is being communicated and to whom it is addressed. Equally important is what the child is hoping to receive back from the adults and how they are going to cope with what they expect to receive. The 5-year-old who has extreme temper tantrums each morning, refusing to go to school, in the hope that he may never have to go to school, is bound to be disappointed!

Control v. Communication?

On the whole, in schools children's behaviour is regarded as something to be controlled. Sally was 5-years old when her mother brought her to see me. She had been in school for just over a term. Each morning began with tears, tantrums and a long list of physical ailments which she felt meant she could not go to school. The parents, and indeed the school, were handling the problem firmly but kindly, insisting that Sally did go to school. She was separated, screaming, from her mother at the classroom door. Often Sally would settle down when her mother left, but then became unreasonably distressed at odd times throughout the day. At times she had been allowed to return home.

Jemma was 6 when she came to see me with her parents. A lively, chatty and spontaneous child at home, she had made no protest about going to school. Although she talked little about school at home, her parents had no reason to be worried until the half-term meeting with teachers. At this meeting a class teacher told the parents that Jemma was withdrawn in class, very quiet, often seen staring into space and did not readily mix with other children. In summary, she seemed to have a secret worry.

The very different behaviours of these two children could be understood as communicating a similar problem.

Looking after the grown-ups

Sally was the youngest of three children, there being a nine-year gap between her and the next child. The parents' marriage had been unhappy for a number of years and both parents had pursued busy careers, perhaps as a way of ignoring the difficulties in their relationship. Sally was cared for by a live-in nanny who had left as she started school, and a new au pair had arrived to stay with the family. What emerged was that Sally had an anxiety that mummy and daddy would be unhappy while she was at school. Much of her behaviour could be understood as a refusal to grow up and become independent. She was refusing to go on to the next stage of her life. This made sense as one understood Sally's perception of her role in the family. Somewhere she had picked up what the parents had verbalised quite openly, 'We are only staying together for the children.' Unconsciously, Sally had an anxiety that if she grew up, there would be no children at home, and her parents would separate.

Do mummy and daddy remember me?

Jemma's story was rather different. The elder of two children, she had a particularly close relationship with her father. This close relationship seemed to have developed over the birth of the second child when Jemma was 2 years old. At that time, due to the mother's ill health, the father had taken over much of the physical care of Jemma. Father worked locally and, until Jemma went to school, he had regular contact with her both by popping into the home during the day and also on the telephone. What emerged was that Jemma somehow felt forgotten at school by her parents. She had little idea that her parents had 'a space in their minds' for her and thought about her when she was not present. Her mother had been hospitalised for some weeks and the phone calls during the day with her father, which were usually initiated by Jemma, seemed to be Jemma's unconscious way of checking that she hadn't been forgotten. When she went to school of course she lost the phone calls.

Jemma's dad comes to the rescue

The difficulties were relatively easily remedied when Jemma's secret worry was brought out into the open and by the parents throwing into the conversation during the evening phrases like 'When I was at work, I was thinking about you and...'

Permission to forget about mum and dad

Jemma was a child who couldn't settle. She feared being forgotten. However, children who settle very well may exhibit similar anxieties. I remember being present in a friend's home when her 5½-year-old came home from school and was sitting having orange juice and a biscuit and was clearly rather down. Her mother noticed and said:

'You seem a bit glum, Mandy.'

'Yes,' she said, and two tears rolled down her cheeks.

'Sometimes when I'm at school, I'm so happy I forget about mummy and daddy.'

Adults always have to remember

Fortunately this mother was quick to reassure the child that although Mandy might forget about her, the job of mothers is to keep remembering their child. Mandy's relatively extreme distress could be understood as an expression of her guilt for forgetting about her parents. Children can feel troubled about forgetting about parents because to them, it feels like an active attack on the parents.

> In children's minds forgetting about a parent and 'getting rid of' or even 'killing off' a parent can easily be confused.

The Child Who Doesn't Learn

A child of good enough ability who seems to settle in school and yet seems unable to make progress academically can be of great concern to parents and teachers alike. Such a child may be a real challenge for the parental expectations discussed earlier. Such a child may also be a real challenge to a teacher – if a child does not learn, then there is an unspoken implication that maybe a teacher is not doing their job.

What does a child need in order to learn?

◆ A secure base from which to venture out into the world.
◆ Permission to be curious.

A secure base

The term 'secure base' was first used by Mary Ainsworth (1967) to describe how a baby uses the mother 'as a secure base from which to explore'. Most children, she believes, get this secure base from the knowledge of being loved by two people who love each other and who love them. These two people, i.e. the parents, or parent substitutes, may not be living together. Separated parents who can convey an ongoing respect and warmth for each other may well provide a secure base. (Where there is overt hostility between separated parents the situation becomes more complex.) This may seem idealised, but, of course, such an ambience in a child's life does not preclude there being difficulties within the family. Being a human being is a messy business and there is nothing which is guaranteed to make a good life. However, when the relationship between the parents is good enough, despite life's ups and downs, then the child can be understood to have an optimum opportunity for learning.

'I think I am a good bloke, therefore I am a good bloke' – Why a secure base is important

♦ A secure base gives a child a sense of good self-esteem, i.e. I am lovable, I am capable.

♦ A secure base encourages a child to achieve, 'When I grow up I will be a daddy, when I grow up I'll be a teacher like mummy, etc, etc.' The child sees advantages in being grown up and acquiring adult skills such as reading and writing.

♦ A secure base allows a child not to be preoccupied with what is in their parents' minds. They are free to be curious about other things.

Children are concerned about what is in their parents' minds, because they are dependent upon them. The more secure a child feels that the adults around them recognise and accept them as a person in their own right, with their own unique way of thinking, feeling and expressing themselves, then the more free they are to learn. It is only when a child is heard and appreciated that they are able to learn. What links a child to the world, to life, to shared experiences, and meaningful relationships, is when what is real to them is real to somebody else.

Permission to be curious

A child needs to feel free to let their mind roam around the questions of their world. This may seem an extraordinary thing to say, and may provoke confusion. When there is a secret in the family, then a child may quickly come to learn not to ask questions about that secret. Eventually it may become impossible for them to question anything, for fear they will discover the thing that musn't be known.

George was 6 when he was referred to me. He was thought to be of gifted intelligence but was making very little headway in school. Something his teachers had noticed, and that his parents confirmed, was that whilst George was able to absorb information very readily, he rarely asked the questions one might expect of a bright child trying to extend his knowledge.

The family picture was complex. The parents were separated, although living under the same roof. Father had a mistress with whom he spent Tuesday and Thursday nights. There were financial reasons why the parents did not want their separation to be made public. The explanation given to George for his father's absences was that 'daddy was at work'. During his pre-school years George had accepted this explanation but when he went to school, and begun to learn more about jobs and the nature of the work, it simply didn't make sense...

> Often when a child appears not to be learning, it can be not so much that the child is failing to learn, but that he has a different agenda, a different curriculum to that of the school.

The child may wish to study 'why dad left home', this may be the area of his curiosity, his maths may be 'what doesn't add up in my life?', his history question, 'why have certain life events happened to me and how much it is my fault?' Michael Eigen talks of the child's 'official' and 'unofficial' development. Officially a child may be expected to follow the school curriculum, unofficially he or she will have their own curriculum to study.

But Where Does the Problem Lie?

Children are sometimes assessed as having a problem in learning or even a learning difficulty, without due regard being given to the different processes in the stages of learning. The parallels between the process of learning and the process of feeding are well documented. One takes something in, makes it one's own, and passes it out in a different form. In thinking about a child not learning, it is important to identify in which process of learning the child is inhibited, the process of taking in information, the process of processing information, or the process of reproducing information in a meaningful form. If you think of all the times that you cannot eat, then you are likely to identify the times when it is difficult for a child to learn.

◆ When there is a physical problem, i.e. the child cannot hear or see properly, or has a specific learning difficulty such as dyslexia.

◆ When the child is in emotional turmoil, for example, if the child has a secret worry or is preoccupied and anxious about unhappinesses in their life.

◆ When the child is simply not hungry – the ability of adults, and other children, to motivate a child to learn cannot be over-emphasised. Nor, indeed, can the impossibility of 'force feeding' a child. Sometimes the child may simply be not hungry. If loss of appetite is the child's way of trying to communicate then it may be almost impossible for adults to motivate them until that communication has been heard.

◆ When the child is already full – the implications of the school time-tabling and excessive parental pressure over homework are obvious.

◆ When the food or the giver of the food is unattractive. When a child has a warm relationship with a stimulating and responsive teacher, in a physically attractive environment with clean and well presented equipment and materials, then you have the optimum situation for learning.

◆ When food has associations. For example some people may associate tomato soup as a comforting winter warming dish, others may associate it with illness, the food that was always offered when they weren't well as a child. A 12-year-old at her first high tea at boarding school was appalled when the pupil sitting next to her said of the poached eggs on toast 'they look like dead eyes'. When a child is asked to read aloud, they are asked to read aloud all their associations with the words and story. A 16-year-old, abused and abandoned by her father, described her difficulty in studying *King Lear* for GCSE. Such perceptions are always idiosyncratic and this is what can make it so difficult to understand another person.

'He simply doesn't listen' – the hyperactive child

'The problem is he just doesn't listen, that's half the problem anyway, you can see he's just not concentrating.'

I have almost come to expect that or a similar line to be included in any description of a child referred to me with distracted and distracting behaviour. Requests for a diagnosis of HADD are very common nowadays and, whilst I am not disputing the authenticity of physical and neurological problems, I am discussing here the emotional basis of poor concentration and hyperactivity and what the child might be communicating by these symptoms. The child who can't stay still, either physically tearing round the classroom or scraping their chair when seated, etc, or who is just restless, jerky or fiddling in class, can be an irritant as well as a cause for concern to both teachers and parents. This is particularly so if the adults have a sense that the child 'won't' rather than 'can't' listen or sit still.

Understanding about my feet

'People don't understand about my feet, my feet keep moving because my head is sad.' (Bereaved 10-year-old)

When asked how they are coping with a trauma or anxiety, adults will quite often say 'Well, I keep busy, I try not to think about it too much.' And so it is for children.

> Keeping busy, trying not to think about something, may be expressed by a child in hyperactivity. Constantly 'on the go', such a child may be avoiding painful and difficult thoughts and feelings as though they could expel them through activity.

Learning becomes practically impossible because most of the child's energy is going into being active. They can't concentrate – because they are working very hard not to concentrate on something!

Who listens to Nora?

Eight-year-old Nora drove both parents and teachers to distraction with her failure to listen. When asked to do something, she would appear to take notice and nod but the task would rarely be completed. My first question about any child so referred is, 'Who listens to her?' We learn to listen by having the experience of being listened to. Nora's parents were appalled to realise how little they listened to her. Both Nora's siblings were in their late teens. At meal times the four adults in the family tended to talk around the table together, throwing the odd kind word and paying lip-service to any real interest in what Nora had to say.

The hopefully depressed

When you are depressed it is likely to be obvious to those around you. You are likely to be listless, lethargic and unmotivated. Children's depression is different from that of adults. The depressed child may be tense, alert, constantly on the go. Why? The depressed child is hoping that someone may hear and understand. The depressed adult often feels hopeless that no one can hear and understand.

> Children's depression is different from adults' in that it is frequently mixed with a persistent hope of recovery.

Giving adults the wrong message

The depressed child's activity may mislead adults, the communication is not clear. The child may be dismissed as 'attention seeking' when, in fact, they may be 'attachment seeking' (Williams).

Hyperactivity can be understood as a failure to attach, i.e. a failure to establish the 'internal' secure base talked of earlier. In the words of a 9-year-old, 'I go out in space, I mean like I'm on the moon, I mean like I'm heavy but I want to be weighted.' This hyperactive boy felt he was dangling, not securely attached to an adult, and therefore unable to explore his environment in a meaningful way – the moon walk was the fun, not the study, part of space travel.

Watch the quiet ones!

However, the hyperactive child may be much more hopeful about their predicament than the depressed child who sits silent and withdrawn at the back of the class. Such a child may not so readily seek to attract the teacher's understanding because they have lost their hope of recovery and ceased to look for helpful adults.

When Anxiety is Helpful

The desire to learn is innate. Curiosity is part of play. Play is about experimenting with different versions of oneself. I have already talked about how children cannot help but be curious about what goes on in their parents' minds. There is a difference between an anxious, preoccupying curiosity and a relatively easy and relaxed curiosity. It could be argued that we only think about our parents when there is a problem! The happy child is free to learn about other things. The child who fails to learn should be understood to be communicating a problem of childhood, and needs to be taken seriously. Understanding 'not learning' as a communication can help to depathologise a child in the sense that the message given is that 'there is nothing wrong with you, but you are trying to tell the adults something.'

Trying New Food – just a taste! – Preparing Children for School

'Tom has an interview at secondary school tomorrow... it's traumatic!'
'Why is it traumatic?'
'He's never been interviewed before.'
'But why is it traumatic?'

(Two mothers overheard on a bus)

Parenting is a paradox. From the moment of birth you are bonding with your child in order that they will feel safe and secure, and close to you, because you are providing them with a secure base. From the moment of birth, you are helping your child to separate from you and to go out into the world to lead their own life. Starting school is a tangible mark of the end of your child's babyhood.

Pause for thought

◆ How do you feel about your child starting school?

'It's strange, you want them to go, you are pleased for them, it's a big step... but you don't want them to go... I know I'm losing control of him...'

The likelihood is that you are ambivalent about your child starting school. It is also likely that your child senses your ambivalence. Your task is to provide a balance between letting the child know that they will be missed, i.e. your day will be different without them, and encouraging them to go out and to tackle this new adventure with enjoyment and confidence. Letting your child know that they will be missed and that you will be thinking about them while they are at school, is a very different matter from conveying you don't know how you are going to cope without them. If, as the mother heard on the bus seems to be conveying, every step outside the home is regarded as fraught or even traumatic, then it is not surprising if the child is very anxious and less likely to cope. On the other hand, if you present your child with clear boundaries, empathy and a good liaison with the child's school, then the optimum conditions are likely for your child to thrive.

Clear boundaries

◆ Remember, your child does not choose to go to school. School is imposed on children by the adults. It may be necessary to explain to your child that they have to go to school and that they will have to go every day until they are 16 years old. One 5-year-old, woken on the second Monday morning of term by her mother with: 'Come on, Sophie, time to get up to go to school,' stared in blank amazement at her mother and said: 'I've been to school.'

◆ Explain to your child that they will come home at the end of every day.

◆ Explain that you will be thinking about them during the day. Explain how you hope they will be getting on happily at school while you are getting on happily at home, looking forward to seeing them in the evening.

Empathy

◆ It is likely that your child is both excited and anxious about going to school. Accept both as ordinary phenomena of childhood. If they seem particularly anxious, explain to them how new beginnings are always both exciting and anxiety provoking. Talk to them about how you felt on your first day at school. Tell them what you will be doing during the day so that they can have a mental picture of your day.

◆ Some children can feel comforted by carrying a tiny toy from home in their pocket or school bag. Equally, a little note from you slipped into his lunch box or school bag can be helpful.

Liaison

◆ Find out as much as possible about your child's school and teacher beforehand. If possible, talk to a parent who already has a child at that school.

◆ Visit the school, initially without your child. If possible observe a class or assembly in action. Talk to the head teacher and to the teachers. Does this school taste good?

◆ It is usual nowadays for children to have a preliminary visit when starting school. Show your child where to hang their coat, where the toilets are, and help them to understand the classroom routine. If children can anticipate what is going to happen next, it can help them feel secure.

Pause for thought

◆ How do you feel about your child's teacher?

Your child will quickly pick up your feelings about your child's class teacher. I remember in my first teaching post, coming into conflict with a 5-year-old boy who eventually burst out: 'Well, anyway, my dad says you're only a chit of a girl.'

It is important to present the class teacher as a caring and approachable person. Explain to your child that if they have a problem at school they can tell the teacher who will try to help them in the same way as mummy does at home.

Home Time

◆ When your child comes home from school, listen to their day. Try not to ask direct questions. Asking children questions can often lead to monosyllabic answers or the answer the child thinks you want, for example: 'Did you

have a good time in the playground?' Your child may feel
that they have to say 'Yes' because they should have had a
good time in the playground, or give a monosyllabic reply
because that answers the question. Phrasing such as 'How
was playtime?' may be more of an invitation to
conversation.

◆ Remember that children can settle into school initially very
well, and then a few weeks into the term, experience
difficulties. It is ordinary for children to begin to have
doubts about an experience which they realise is now a
reality. It may be fun and exciting to go to school for a few
weeks, it may become more of an anxiety when you realise
the length of the sentence!

'Freedom comes slowly at first' (Keenan)

◆ What are you, as a parent, going to do when your child goes
to school?

One of the interesting aspects of having a child is that the
child organises your life for you. Having your life organised for
you can lead to a fear of freedom. Some mothers have
described their separation from their child when they go to
school as 'a rupture'. Your child has gone to school, you are
now thrown back on yourself, what do you want to do with the
time? Your child now has another occupation and this gives
you potential mental freedom.

The Cult of Maternal Business

Mothers often described to me how they seem to have no less
time once the child has gone to school. School run, household
chores, dog walking, etc. all seem to fill the time before the
final school run of the day. The danger is that as a mother you
can spend your day waiting for the child to return from school.
There is a sense, of course, in which you will always do so. It is
a shame if child-caring time completely fills the hours that the
child is not at home. It is important to acknowledge that you
and your child are beginning to separate. You now have the
mental freedom to begin to think and plan occupations for
yourself. Younger children, work outside the home, etc, may

give you relatively little physical spare time, but you can begin to think about being other versions of yourself than a parent.

Finally, be aware of Chinese whispers!

When I was teaching, I always ended my welcome to new parents with a promise – 'We won't believe a word they say about you, if you don't believe a word they say about us.'

Children's reports of what happens at school are often akin to a game of Chinese whispers. If what you hear worries you, try not to overreact, but to enquire gently of the class teacher. It is more constructive to take issues up as they arise rather than let them build up as anxieties in your mind.

Summary

- Your attitude to your child's teacher and school will be influenced inevitably by your own school experiences. What can be guaranteed is that your worst experience at school will become your preoccupation at your child's school gates.
- You can help your child's transition from home to school by careful preparation.
- Some children may fear they are forgotten by parents whilst they are at school.
- Some children may need permission to forget about their parents while they are at school.
- In order to learn, a child needs a) a secure base from which to venture out into the world, and b) permission to be curious.
- Often when a child appears not to be learning, it can be not so much that the child is failing to learn, but that they have a different agenda, a different curriculum to that of the school.
- Sometimes hyperactivity can be understood as a failure to attach.
- Children learn to listen by being listened to.
- Both teachers and parents may find it difficult to recognise when a child is depressed. Children's depression is different from adults' in that it is frequently mixed with a persistent hope of recovery.
- How are you going to use your time now that your child is at school?

CHAPTER 6

Believing in Goodness – The Impact of Divorce

Divorce raises many questions both for the children and the adults involved; maybe the most challenging and creative question for parents is 'How can we help the children to make the best of it?'

'Mum and dad have cut up...(pause)...(confused shaking of the head)...I mean, I mean...(sudden recollection)...split up.'

(Six-year-old David)

David stared at me with puzzled satisfaction. At 6 years old he had got the phrase right, the experience remained bewildering and painful – but not only for him, his parents were just as likely to feel 'cut up' as well as 'split up'.

In the previous chapter I talked of the child's need for a 'secure base' from which to explore the world, physically, mentally and emotionally. Traditionally, and perhaps idealistically, the secure base has been understood as two parents who love each other and love the child. But families nowadays are very variable – single parents, step-parents, couples parenting but not living together, gay couples parenting, grandparents or other relatives parenting, and these relationships are becoming increasingly recognised as equal to the traditional idea of the family in terms of providing the child with 'a secure base'. The shattering of this 'secure base' by death, illness, separation or divorce, can be potentially catastrophic for both adults and children involved. Both may experience a sense of bewilderment and disorientation that feels like living on sand.

> Something that everybody, but particularly the children, took for granted and permanent has turned out not to be so.

Nine-year-old Dora's parents had separated and divorced when she was 5 years old. Both had quickly remarried, to spouses with their own children. Within two years both parents had further children with their new spouse. By the time Dora and I met she had nine assorted siblings, step-siblings and half-siblings. Her parents lived in different parts of the country, and access visits were almost inevitably difficult to arrange and chaotic in execution. Juggling the life of a complicated family was a tour de force in planning. Dora felt she had somehow 'got lost' in it all. Visits to her father often had to be cancelled at the last minute; on one occasion he had failed to arrive at the designated service station meeting point, and Dora and her mother had to return home, having waited over an hour. There was a sound and simple explanation but understandably Dora, already insecure of her father's love and attention, felt abandoned and unable to understand the complexity of life for her parents.

She had been seeing me for about six months, a quiet, reserved child, with little eye contact, who seemed suspicious of my attempts to understand her predicament. One week her mother asked to change her next appointment from early morning to lunchtime and I agreed. In the meantime the mother, having forgotten the rearrangement, turned up with Dora at her usual time to find the consulting room empty and locked. She then quickly remembered, explained to Dora, and returned later. Dora told me how disappointed she had been when I was not there when she arrived.

'I thought you'd gone shopping...and...forgotten me.'

'And how did you feel when mummy explained?'

'Good, I felt good, cos you hadn't (forgotten).'

'So how does it feel to have that good feeling that I didn't forget you?'

Dora slowly looked up and stared into my eyes.

'I don't believe in goodness, Mrs Clifford – it doesn't work.'

A Shattered 'Secure Base'

Couples in a painful crisis themselves may find it unbearable to witness, think about and tolerate their children's pain.

A mother, whose husband left 'out of the blue' one weekend, described how she found her 4-year-old, lying on the floor shouting 'I want daddy, I want daddy', and overwhelmed by her own distress, was only able to respond in a disciplinarian way, 'Get up at once, you are just upsetting yourself.' Such a parent may well find trying to establish another kind of secure base for her children impossibly daunting. But the success of the variety of 'families' in the nineties gives us both optimism and sometimes perhaps, models for the restructuring of a new, strange and yet familiar secure base for the children of divorcing parents.

As a therapist working with families pre, post and during divorce, I am only too aware that it is almost impossible to give parents any support in remaining together as a parental couple, as opposed to a sexual couple, without increasing their guilt and anxiety about the children. Offering help in remaining together as a parental couple can imply that it is not in the children's interests for them to split up! But it is not the role of the therapist to keep families together, rather, more importantly, it is to help them to find out how they want to be together and ways in which this can be managed.

> It is important to remember that marriage does not necessarily equate with 'family' or 'home'. These are three separate ideas which may often overlap and interlink and which may be able to exist independently as well.

'It's not their fault, they are just the victims in all this.'
(Divorcing father of three.)

Does being powerless in the face of a life event, as children are in divorce, necessarily mean being a victim? It can be argued that it is not what happens to us in life that matters, but the choices we make in response to life events.

A Failed Relationship?

A 43-year-old divorced father was reflecting upon his very new current relationship. Married twice, once in his 20s, again in his 30s, he had not had a sexual relationship for six years but was now very attracted to a younger woman in his office, who certainly seemed to reciprocate his feelings. He summed up his anxiety and reluctance 'to get involved'.

'I can't face another failed relationship.'

A teenager was discussing her relationship with her first boyfriend which had clearly now run its course. Asked what was stopping her from finishing it she responded 'Then I'll have a failed relationship behind me.'

If problems hunt in pairs, then so do feelings. Divorce seems to be inevitably accompanied by a sense of failure and lack of self-esteem.

◆ Relationships do not fail; they begin, evolve and end.

◆ Marriages do not fail, they begin, usually with high hopes and expectations, they evolve, usually with a fair degree of chaos, and they end, sometimes prematurely and unexpectedly by death or divorce.

◆ It can be argued that the way adults think about their experience of divorce will influence their ability to help their children to 'make the best of it'.

It is often extremely sad, painful, and disappointing when plans made for and within a relationship do not work out. I once asked a young mother who became severely depressed following her divorce, and who felt a keen sense of failure, 'If you weren't feeling a failure, what might you be feeling?'

'Disappointed,' she sobbed, 'so disappointed.'

> It may not be possible to avoid painful disappointment in divorce. There are other ways of thinking about divorce rather than in terms of success and failure.

There is all the difference in these two ways of thinking:

◆ 'Where did I go wrong? I'm a bad wife, a bad mother. I guess that makes me a bad woman.'

and

◆ 'It's (the divorce) not what we planned, we'd rather it hadn't happened, but it has, we'll have to make the best of it, no, make something of it . . . but I guess we both wish it was different.'

What Shall We Tell the Children?

◆ It is best if you tell your children together that you are going to separate. This will reinforce for them that you may be

intending to stay together as 'a parental couple' if not as
lovers.

♦ At the same time, it is important for you to realise that for
your child there may be no acceptable reason for your
separation.

It just doesn't make sense

Out shopping in a busy high street I came across three girls in
a shop doorway. The two older ones, aged possibly 9 and 11
years old, were casting anxious looks at a younger one, aged 4
or 5 years old, who was sobbing bitterly. As I approached the
shop door my eyes met the older girl's. I asked what was the
matter. They looked embarrassed, awkward, as the younger one
sobbed 'Daddy doesn't love mummy any more.'

'I'm sure he loves you.' I reached to comfort her.

'No,' she sobbed, 'No, he'd stay...'

Twelve-year-old Tom was devastated when his parents
separated. A rather formal family, his parents led very separate
lives with Tom at boarding school, but had maintained a
seemingly happy enough home for him during holidays. He
had no inkling of the deep unhappiness in their marriage.

'They say they like each other, but they don't love each
other. They say they don't like each other enough to live
together, so I have to take turns with the holidays. I'll always
be only a little of myself now.'

> In order to make sense of emotional experiences, children
> need to be told the facts.

The two children above had little conscious idea of the
impending break up, their shock and disbelief are evident. In
both cases the parents had tried to explain simply and honestly
that they no longer wished to live together but that they both
continued to love the child. To these children, this simply did
not make sense.

♦ Remember, a parent is part of a child. It is common in
child abuse cases for the child victims to cover for and
defend the abusing parent, often to the surprise of the
investigating adults. If children admit to themselves that one

or both of their parents are 'bad', then they run the risk of acknowledging that part of them is bad.

◆ In the same way, if 'Daddy doesn't love mummy any more' then the child fears that he doesn't love part of the child any more. As a 7-year-old said, 'Maybe I smell, I put my mum's perfume on, but maybe I smell...'

'What will happen to me now?' Honesty is the best policy

◆ When you try to explain to children why you are separating, be as honest and as simple as possible. 'Daddy doesn't love mummy any more; he still really likes her, but he's met somebody else he would like to live with now' may be initially less wounding to a child than a bald statement that one parent simply doesn't love the other any more.

◆ It is important to tell the children that you know they cannot understand why this is happening, and to acknowledge and hold their feelings of both panic and bewilderment.

◆ Your child is likely to be shocked and bewildered. They are likely to express this with two questions: 'What has happened?' and 'What will happen to me now?'

'It's not your fault' adult business

◆ Your child needs a clear, direct message – 'It's not your fault, it was nothing to do with you, this is adult business.' They may feel powerless and angry at such a message, but they will also feel relieved of an unnecessary burden.

◆ Your child's pain may not be avoided, but it can be relieved rather than exaggerated. The 4-year-old who asks: 'Why doesn't daddy come to see me?' is not helped by the desperate and abandoned mother who responds, 'Because he doesn't want to see us, there is nothing I can do.'

> Despite your mixed and confusing feelings at this time, what your child needs, most of all, is to be reassured that both parents still love him, that both will continue to want to see him and, perhaps most importantly, that he is not going to be asked to choose between his parents.

Goodbye makes us sad and angry

Sometimes a parent leaves suddenly or hostilely. There may be no opportunity to prepare the children. Sometimes it is known at the time of the separation that the departing parent is unlikely to have much contact with the child. The remaining parent has a formidable task. Children cannot be expected to think rationally when their whole world has been turned upside down. The remaining parent is left to soak up the child's pain, anger, disappointment, and sense of abandonment.

'It's not fair...it's their mother who's left...but I get all the bad behaviour...you'd think it was my fault.' (Divorced father of two.)

Children may be afraid of being angry with the departed parent for fear of keeping them away!

Daddy leaves home

'If I get angry with daddy, he might not come back'

'I must have been naughty. Daddy has gone 'cos he's angry with me'

'I feel angry with daddy for going'

> Sometimes it is most helpful not to offer explanations or excuses for the absent parent, but to simply accept how the child feels, for instance, 'It makes you sad and angry when daddy isn't in touch.'

'Particular to Thee' – the Unique Experience

Murray Cox has highlighted the scene in *Hamlet* where the prince is beginning to go mad following his father's death. His mother, Gertrude, tries to comfort him. She points out that many young men of Hamlet's age lose their father and recover without falling apart in the way Hamlet seems to be doing. She adds:

'Why seems this so particular with thee?'
'Nay, madam, I know not seems, it is.'

It is interesting how in families siblings are often referred to by a collective noun, 'the children' or 'the girls' or 'the boys', 'the twins', 'the little ones', or as an overwhelmed father of four used to say 'that lot'. At one level this is understandable, but at another it emphasises the thought I raised earlier, that in distress it is often hard for the adults to recognise 'the particular' for each child. Adults tend to speak of how 'the children' are reacting.

◆ There are as many experiences of divorce as there are people experiencing divorce.

◆ In my clinical experience, whilst there are common themes for all children, it is also a unique experience. Some children will seem to take the matter in their stride, others may be inconsolable.

Perhaps one of the difficult tasks for parents is trying to accommodate this fact in a family. Trying to hold in mind the 'particular' for each child is demanding and stressful at a time when parental resources may be low. It may be easier to think of the reactions of 'the children' in a blanket way.

Peter, Philip and Jane

Peter, Philip and Jane came to see me with their father 18 months after their parents had divorced. Initially the parents had 'shared the care', the children living with their mother during the week, their father at the weekends. A year later the mother was offered promotion at work which meant a change of location, and the father decided to remarry. It was thought to be in the children's best interests now to be with their father during the term time and spend their holidays with their mother.

Peter and Jane seemed to have negotiated this upheaval in their lives. Initially distressed at the break-up of the family home, they settled quickly into the new routine. In common with many children, Peter and Jane were greatly helped to settle by the fact that they felt genuinely wanted in both their parents' homes. They were anxious and upset when the arrangements changed again and their mother moved away. However, they seemed contained by daily phone calls and the odd weekend visit when it could be arranged.

'The "problem" was Philip'

At the time of the separation Philip, aged 8, had been distraught. An extrovert child, he had many interests, cubs, gym club, etc which he promptly refused to attend, eventually sobbing, 'I don't want people to know my family have split up.' He became quiet and withdrawn, sleeping and eating poorly and his school work suffered.

As the months went by he seemed to adapt to the initial new regime, but would cling to his mother on Friday evenings when she left and to his father on Sunday evenings when he left. His mother described him 'as going through the motions, not really seeming to enjoy or dislike anything.'

A year later when the new living arrangements came into being, Philip began to petty pilfer, first from home, then from school, and eventually from the local shops, precipitating his referral to me. Philip's parents had tried hard to understand and comfort him. They were puzzled why he had been so affected, wondering if it was connected with 'middle child syndrome'. They were relieved the other children had reacted so relatively well, and felt a mixture of guilt and frustration over Philip.

'Philip's upset, 'cos he misses his mum'

At the beginning of the family session, Peter and Jane were quick to volunteer they had all come to see me ''Cos of Philip, he's naughty' which later became 'Philip's upset, 'cos he misses mum'.

'Is it only Philip who misses mum?' I asked.

'Yes,' said Peter quickly, 'well ... no ... not really ...,' he swallowed hard, 'but Philip misses mum.'

Maybe Peter was giving us a clue!

> Sometimes one child can carry all the distress, grief and anxiety for the other children. By becoming 'the unhappy one' (or even 'the happy one') in the family, the other children can be freed to get on with their lives. There is a sense in which Philip was freed to feel grief. His brother and sister were freed from grief.

Peter and Jane didn't need to think about the less satisfactory aspects of their parents' divorce as Philip was doing it for them. As time went on, the balance was redressed with Peter and Jane feeling a little more sad, freeing Philip from his role of 'the problem' and he began to enjoy life a little more. Peter was able to volunteer that as the eldest child he felt he had to keep his sadness 'a secret – in case the others get more upset', and Jane said 'I'm not sad, 'cos if I think about my mum, I'm sad, so I don't think about it.'

'So how do you feel when you see Philip sad?'

'Well, 'cos, that's Philip missing his mum...'

'His mum?'

'My mum too,' she said quietly and sadly.

At a follow-up appointment eight months later, it was interesting to see how well the family was coping. Now that everybody was 'feeling their own feelings' as Peter put it, life seemed more manageable and happy for everyone.

A Kind of Bereavement?

'I go into the bathroom, 'cos it smells of his (the father's) aftershave, and I smell it when I'm sad.'

No one could have failed to have been moved by the 10-year-old in the television documentary describing her feelings of loss after her father left home. The picture she painted of herself, missing her father, and going into the bathroom to smell his aftershave in order to feel close to him, was that of a bereaved child.

For both adults and children, the experience of divorce may be very similar to that of bereavement, but the two are like and unlike. They have in common the fact that the child has to realise that things have changed irrevocably – and nothing will ever be the same again. Not only has their security been shattered, but for most children their worst fears will have come true.

'They rowed and rowed and I used to wish they'd separate, I used to wish my dad would go, and then they'd stop having rows...but I never meant it, I never meant it' – a 9-year-old sobs when she talks of her parents' impending separation.

In coming to terms with this fact, the feelings may be the

same in both divorce and death but the life tasks involved are different.

> 'So I said to them, "I don't know why you two don't separate, you're always fighting, you'd be better off apart." I didn't think they'd do it, I just couldn't stand it.'
>
> A 12-year-old talks of how although he longed for his parents' separation at times, for him it came out of the blue when it happened.

At this time children may feel that they have lost a parent, but it is also very common for the parent with whom the child does not reside, to feel that they have 'lost' their child, particularly if a step-parent is heavily involved in parenting.

When a parent dies the child has to come to terms with the fact that they will never see the parent again. Even in religious households, where belief in an afterlife may be prevalent, it would be unusual to lead the child to believe that after death the relationship will be exactly the same as it was in life. Rituals such as the funeral help the child to say goodbye and to accept the finality of death.

In the months following the death the child may be encouraged to 'let go' of the dead parent mentally and re-build their own life in which the deceased has an integral but historical part.

'Neil lives with mummy now...'

In divorce, the child has to negotiate a different kind of being together with the departed parent.

'When I go to stay with mummy I sleep in the big bed with her. I expect Neil will sleep in the settee.' (6-year old girl).

Needless to say this child had much to struggle with when she found Neil was to share the big bed and she herself was 'in the settee'. In divorce, the sense of loss may feel as acute as if the parent has died. However, your child should not be encouraged to 'let go' of the departed parent. Your children need to be encouraged to establish a new 'way' of having a relationship. Your child may feel as though they have to establish 'a new relationship'. It is important to remind the child that the fundamental relationship is the same. It is the way of having that relationship that is different.

When Daddy Doesn't Visit

'My daddy doesn't come to see us any more, my daddy's forgotten all about us now.' (4-year-old.)

Sometimes divorce will mean that the child has to negotiate the fact that the parent may choose not to see them.

If you can manage to make the new living and access arrangements for the children both tolerable and reliable, then your children are likely to cope.

> The advantage of reliability is that when children are not preoccupied with anxieties about when they may see the other parent, they seem to be able to live in the present and to adapt to their new situation.

Things become more complicated when there is overt hostility between the parents.

The Child as a Weapon

Mr and Mrs A had decided to separate after nine years of marriage because of the husband's 'serial adultery'. Mrs A had frequently given him 'another chance' but had come to understand her husband's affairs as a symbol of his general reluctance to take on the responsibilities of family life. She felt he took less than his fair share of the tasks of home and child-care. Commuting to work, he frequently entertained clients in the city after work, arriving home in the early hours of the morning somewhat intoxicated. Sometimes he wouldn't come home, spending ill-afforded money on hotel bills.

He would often not come to see the mother and two children from one weekend to the next. At the time the parents sought my help, the husband was about to move in with his current girlfriend, the family home was to be sold, the mother and children moving into a smaller property.

Both parents were anxious to handle the telling of the children in as constructive a manner as possible. In a discussion on access arrangements, the mother insisted she would not allow the children to meet her husband's girlfriend or to go to their shared home. As we unravelled this objection, she was appalled to realise that it was partly a way of getting back at her husband. She knew he had little idea of how to entertain the children. By limiting access to treat days out and no overnight stays, she was restricting their relationship with their father. She quickly admitted her wish to punish him for his behaviour, but had not realised that she was asking her children to pay the price.

However, even in the best-regulated divorced households, children have to process overt or covert bitterness in the adults' relationship. It can be very difficult for a mother, receiving inadequate basic maintenance, not to communicate resentment as her children gleefully recount the extravagant expensive treats they have had with their father at the weekend. Most poignant is the single mother who has saved hard to buy her child a much coveted toy for Christmas, only to have the child return from a pre-Christmas visit to her father clutching the same!

The Stages of Development

Children's reactions to divorce will depend on both their personality and their family relationships. They will also respond differently according to their developmental age.

Three-years-old and under

For children under 3 years the most important developmental task is that of consolidating a sense of being attached to a 'good enough' parent, in other words, toddlers are establishing their notion of a 'secure base'. They are age-appropriately anxious and insecure when separated from their parents – a 3-year-old on a family outing may revel in the company of a doting aunt, but will often 'just go back and see my mummy' – a sort of quick check that her anchor and reference point has not disappeared. This is very different from the 3-year-old, a year after her parents' separation, who became highly anxious and insecure whenever she left the security of the family home. Visits to someone as familiar as her grandmother always began with her being dragged screaming from the car, and then hysterically trying to get out of the house, sobbing, 'I want to go home, I want to go home.' She calmed down unusually quickly one day when a visitor commented quietly, 'You can go home, Jane, you can go home, when we've all had tea.'

This child's security seemed to have been shattered to such a degree that she only felt safe with her mother in their own four walls. The 'secure base' was very much a physical one.

As I have already discussed, often the hardest part of divorce for children is that something they had taken as permanent and for granted, turned out not to be so. Their capacity to deal with the unexpected may be temporarily, but not necessarily permanently, limited and fragile.

Like all children her age, at the time of the separation, Jane needed her mother to reinforce her sense of belonging, not only by her reassuring presence, but by keeping her in a regular routine. In this way Jane began to build up a sense of security by being able to sequence and predict her life – 'After lunch, we'll go to the park, and then we'll come home for tea.'

Telling the child the story of her life may also help. Children love to hear their 'own story', how they were born, christened, etc. A sense of history will help the child to feel anchored in the present and able to venture into the future.

Four-to-7-years-old – a child blames themself

'I wouldn't do my homework and I kept having argues with my sister and that... I expect that's why.'

Ian was a belligerent and unhappy 9-year-old, described by his teachers as 'always at the centre of trouble.' His father had found it hard to sole parent Ian and his sister. He was puzzled by Ian's troublesome behaviour. 'He knows he can't get away with it, he knows he'll get caught.'

When I asked Ian why he thought his mother had left home, he thought for a while and said, 'I didn't behave...like I was noisy.'

At the time of the separation, Ian had been given the reasons for his mother's departure. However, to him it seemed inexplicable and in spite of being given the facts, he had formulated his own reasons. In previous chapters I have talked of how children at certain ages, tend to see themselves as the centre of their world, and to presume they are the cause or the effect of all their life events. Ian's difficult behaviours could be understood as his asking the adults a question, 'Was this why she left, is this what I did? Is this what happened?' The more he was punished, the more 'bad' he felt. Ian's father had to work hard at reiterating the clear message, 'It was not your fault, it was nothing to do with you, this was adult business.'

Eight-to-eleven-years-old – 'I just wanted to be an ordinary girl'

Eight-year old Carol was angry! Her anger spilled into every part of her life. Doors were kicked open, slammed, shoes were hurled into cupboards, food gobbled at high speed. The slightest frustration was met with violent outbursts of temper. Her mother described her as having 'a permanent discontented look.' Carol's parents separated when she was 7. Her father's job had taken him increasingly away from home and the parents 'lost track of each other', and both developed new relationships. Carol deeply resented both new partners and her mother's boyfriend had eventually moved out of the home 6 months prior to our meeting.

She spent the weekends with her father who lavished her with expensive gifts and outings, but she was no less angry in his home than in that of her much less wealthy mother.

Initially her parents thought she would settle down as time went by. However, as her behaviour continued to cause concern over a year after the separation, her mother sought professional help.

The mother was clearly feeling hopeless and inadequate in my first meeting with them. She listed anxiously all she had tried to do for Carol. She described the father's indulgence of her, and finished rather lamely, 'We can't do anything right, we don't know what she wants.' Carol, who up until then had sat glowering in her chair, interrupted angrily, 'I want to be an ordinary girl, in an ordinary family – I just want a mum and dad living together like everyone else.'

The importance of comparisons

'It's not fair, it's not fair, I don't want people to know my home is split up, it's not fair,' cried one 9-year-old. Children of this age may be preoccupied with comparisons, who has what, and where they fit into the pecking order. Often the impact of divorce is reflected in such children's preoccupation. Whilst they may experience their share of guilt and sadness, it can be that the impact of the divorce will predominantly be a sense of rage and injustice. Even in an age where divorce is such a relatively common event, such children may feel that they have been singled out for a raw deal.

Children of this age need time, space and permission to be angry but they also need help in keeping their anger focused.

Carol found it easier to contain her anger when her mother adopted a more reflective approach. For example, when Carol flew into a rage over fish fingers rather than sausages for tea, her mother would calmly and firmly say: 'Carol, you're angry that daddy and I don't live together, not that you're having sausages rather than fish fingers for tea.' Such reflection seemed to help her understand that however much she protested, she could not influence the situation. In common with many children of divorced parents, Carol was harbouring a persistent hope that her parents would get back together.

Nine-year-old Mark caused his mother some concern in the months following his father's sudden departure by his increasingly seemingly insatiable material desires. His demands for, and protestations that he was entitled to, an excessive amount of presents, toys, new clothes and even food, was typified on the day he returned from a trip to the local fair with a schoolfriend. Aware of the family's reduced income, the schoolfriend's father had lavished Mark with spoils from the fair. He came home, hugging his toys more in a sense of greed and possessiveness than in glee and satisfaction.

'Goodness, what a lot of toys, there can't be many boys of 9 who got so much from the fair,' his mother said.

'No,' he responded, 'and their dads haven't left home either.'

Mark's behaviour could be understood as a way of telling his mother that he felt deprived, deprived of the father he had so adored. His sense of injustice, his constant feeling 'this is not fair', was leading him to believe that not only was he entitled to more material goods than other children, but that possessions could in some way compensate for his loss.

Twelve-plus years – 'I'd rather not have a party' – grief and loss

Twelve-year-old Simon's mother left home a week after his birthday. As his 13th birthday approached he refused any offer of a celebration suggested by his father, however tempting. Initially he would not give a reason, just a shrug of the shoulders accompanied by, 'I'd rather not have a party.' Then one day he broke down sobbing, 'My mum always did it (the party), and now she's not here.'

This sensitive father was quick to suggest a few away-days away for his birthday, placing it in a different context from those previously. He made no attempt to 'cheer Simon up', but accepted how painful and difficult it was for him this year and helped him to find another way of having a birthday. Young teenagers are more capable of verbalising their feelings than younger children. However, this may not preclude them from falling back on behaviour as a communication.

Social and Political Factors

'But it's not just sad and angry, it's about not having things...it's about the other kids...'

A 10-year-old boy raged week after week to me about his father's departure. I thought it most important to let him rage and help him to connect this rage with his equally deep-felt sadness. He had been describing a row with his mother on return from a weekend visit to his father. It seemed obvious to me that the mother had been the butt of his misplaced anger towards his father. I reflected, 'Goodbye makes us sad and angry.'

He was quick to remind me that it was not only feelings that he had to negotiate. He had swapped a certain and stable emotional life for a more precarious one. He now felt out of control and had divided loyalties with his parents. He also had swapped a financially secure and generous lifestyle for a much more meagre one. The family home – the only home he had known – had been sold, and he and his mother had moved to a much smaller house in a less affluent area. He understood well the link between his loss of social status and his increasing loss of self-esteem. He saw himself as 'different' from his other friends, and 'less good' than they, because of his lack of expensive games and designer clothes.

He had suddenly become a member of a 'one parent family'. He was having to deal not only with 'the particular' of that for him, but also with how such a family is construed in society. His mother was in the habit of listening to Radio 4 in the mornings. One day, at breakfast, he suddenly asked, 'Mummy, do we get benefits?' He was beginning to fear that he and his family were cast in a group portrayed less than sympathetically by the media.

How Parents Can Help

'I know I'm doing the right thing, we can't go on suffocating each other like this, but the kids ... they're devastated ... we're wrecking their lives.' (Divorcing father.)

Most parents going through divorce are likely to express, at some time or other, that they or would have liked to stay together for the sake of the children. Sometimes parents seeking help with their relationship will state that as the reason they are still together. I am always suspicious when that reason is given.

> Couples find all sorts of reasons for staying together and separating. Couples do not stay together for the children; the children in such cases are invariably 'a mask' for other reasons the couple are together. 'Staying together because of the children' can be a way of not thinking about other reasons a couple want to be together.

The other side of divorce is that however willing both parties might be to try, sometimes relationships do not work. Being a human being is a messy business and cannot be ordered or controlled always by an act of will. In my clinical experience, parents seeking help with divorce tend to fall into two ways of thinking:

◆ They are over-anxious about the effect on the children
◆ They are dismissive of the effect on the children.

Attributing every undesirable aspect of a child's behaviour to 'reaction to the divorce' may be as unhelpful as asserting boldly that the children have not been affected or are even much happier. Of course there are extremes of behaviour both ways – the traumatised child and the child who seems more content because they are not living in a war zone.

The difficult balancing act for you, as parents, lies in being able to acknowledge that your actions have had an impact on the child, but also knowing that beating yourself up on this matter will not help you to bear the child's confusion and pain. In such crisis times, thinking in terms of right and wrong may be less productive than thinking in terms of behaviour and consequences. If you divorce there will be one set of consequences for the children. If you stay together, there will be another set.

> Nobody chooses their parents, we take what we get and make the best of it.

So how can parents help children to make the best of it, to keep alive the fact of the separation and yet not let it spoil everything? Believing they can must be half the battle, for such parents convey to the child consciously and unconsciously 'this is difficult but it can be okay' – a very different message from 'this is terrible and it's all our fault you are miserable.' Whilst no child should ever feel responsible for their parents, children can be helped in times of crisis to feel that they can contribute something reparative to the situation. A child may feel less out of control and bewildered if there is a sense of the family sharing the project of how to deal with this new crisis.

'I feel like a Christmas cracker' – on not drawing children into parents' hostilities

I have already mentioned the paradoxical importance of children not being drawn into adult conflicts. Of course there is a sense in which they always are, but parents can take conscious steps to limit the amount.

Eleven-year-old Tom was about to spend Easter with his

father and step-family. Half an hour before he was due to leave
he announced he had to go to the high street to buy an Easter
present for his father. Knowing there was insufficient time for
this, Tom's mother was immediately put in a dilemma. If she
agreed the father would be kept waiting at the meeting point
with two small step-children. She tried to persuade Tom this
wasn't essential, dad would be just as pleased to see him, but
to no avail, and in the end she agreed to the high street visit.

In recounting the episode, she said, 'Of course, I realised I
was really fed up because he hadn't bought me an Easter
present, why should his dad get one!' A rather poignant ending
to this story was that Tom had chosen a *Beano* book for his
father and was overwhelmed with joy on Easter morning when
he found dad had bought him the same one. 'He bought me
the very same, mum, he bought me the very same, we are dead
alike.'

It can be very difficult for the parent who has custody to
tolerate the seeming idealisation of the other parent – as one
child described it 'Santa Claus Daddy'. At such times it is
essential that parents hold onto the fact as this mother did, that
the child is likely to feel less secure with the parent he visits
and he may be afraid of being angry or disruptive with that
parent for fear of driving them further away. As a 10-year-old
said, 'I try hard at dad's, I don't want to let him down, I don't
want him to be disappointed 'cos ...'cos ... I have to be his
best son.'

When it's all right to be unhappy

Crucial in this process is the parents' understanding of the
child's behaviour prior to and following visits. When Tom was
5, access visits always ended with Tom having nightmares the
last night at his father's and the first night back at his mother's.
His father construed this as Tom being happier with him and
not wanting to return to his mother. The mother construed it
that the access visits were upsetting Tom and needed to be
curtailed. Fortunately, both resisted the temptation to blame
each other and were helped to understand that the problem
was Tom's struggle to cope with the transition from one parent
to another. He needed to be reassured by both parents that

they were pleased to see him and would hold him in mind in his absence.

Keeping mum and dad together in my mind

'On Saturday I went to Cubs' party and mummy went out with her friend, and on Sunday I played football with James, and mummy went shopping for a party dress for next week.' Tom's mother was describing her frustration at her loss of a private life. Her children telephoned their father every day and would recount not only their activities, but also hers, in great detail. When they stayed with their father, they did the same about his life.

'I know,' said the mother, 'I know it would be disastrous for me to tell him not to tell his father what I am doing, but I'm fed up with it.' She was able to appreciate that what Tom was trying to do was to keep his parents together as a couple in his mind, even if they were separated physically. To ask him to limit what he said to either parent would be to draw him into their hostility and run the risk of his feeling more of a 'Christmas cracker'. Fortunately for Tom, his divorced parents had learned a crucial lesson early on in their attempts to remain together as a 'parental couple'.

Don't mix facts and feelings

'I don't know what happened, I just phoned to discuss which weekends he (Tom's father) wanted the children next term. He kept saying, 'Well, I'm away that weekend' or 'We've got theatre tickets that weekend' and we ended up having a blazing row. I pointed out I wished that I was free to make social arrangements.'

It may seem obvious, and rather artificial, to suggest parents try to keep the making of formal arrangements for the children, money, etc separate from conversations about feelings. Conversations over practical matters are potentially emotionally highly charged, with a covert agenda of anger, resentment and guilt. It could be argued that it is almost impossible to have a conversation to arrange for a child to see one of their parents without both parents feeling guilty and upset that they have created this situation for the child.

◆ Some parents find it more straightforward to make arrangements in writing. When feelings are flying high, it is easy to mishear or misconstrue not only words, but tone of voice; writing it down can help to avoid misunderstanding and confusion.

◆ Letters to be delivered by the child need to be handed over with a pleasant and constructive, 'Would you give this to daddy, it's about your next visit', rather than a somewhat angrier, 'Give this to your father', which may consolidate the child's anxiety about having parents who dislike each other enough not to be able to speak to each other.

The importance of reliability and consistency

'My dad's taking me skiing at Christmas, it'll be really good, my dad's going to teach me to ski.'

'Has dad said that?'

'Yes.'

'Recently?'

'Yes, my dad's taking me skiing.'

'Sometimes dad has good ideas but then he can't always do it.'

'If he doesn't do this then I'll kill him, this'll be his last chance, I'll kill him.'

This conversation between a 9-year-old and her mother was painful to witness. The mother knew the father was going to renege on his promise and was struggling both to let the child down gently and also to persuade the father to tell her sooner rather than later.

> Whilst consistency and reliability are always essential elements of parenting, they become of prime importance following a divorce. Parents need to keep reminding children that they want to see them and to be scrupulous in keeping arrangements.

◆ Generally speaking, an arrangement with the child has to take priority in the parent's life.

◆ If for any reason it has to be cancelled, the child will need not only a careful explanation and reassurance of the parent's disappointment, but also an opportunity to express their feelings – sadness, disappointment, anger, resentment, rejection, etc to both parents.

◆ At such a time a factual argument, 'I had to work, I'm really sorry', may be essential at the outset, but what the child also needs is a message that the parent understands how he feels, not just a justification of what has happened.

◆ Remember, to the child there may be no explanation good enough for a cancelled access visit.

Nine-year-old Morag lived with her mother in Scotland. Her father and his new family had moved to London when she was 4 years old. Money was limited, and for various reasons access visits difficult to arrange, but every summer Morag spent two weeks with her father. For three years this had been the only time she had seen him, though he kept in touch by phone and letter. One summer he was unable to have her for a variety of complicated matters in his current family. He was as distraught as Morag about the matter, but attempts to console her on the phone turned into rows and tantrums as he persisted with factual information, feeling increasingly guilty and defensive in the face of her distress.

'Daddy doesn't love me,' she sobbed, 'he doesn't, or he'd come and see me. He'd let me go if he wanted to see me.'

Morag's father was encouraged to absorb her pain and anger and not to defend against it, by explaining it away with the facts of the situation. She was able to have more sense of being held in mind by him, more connected to him. Morag's rage gave way to sadness. For both her parents, it was a harrowing experience. However, they were both able to help her make the best of it by accepting and sharing her feelings. Her mother arranged other enjoyable treats for the holiday without trying to pretend they were the same or as good as visiting daddy.

The less you had the more you need

Millie's mother was an air hostess who was frequently away from home, leaving Millie to be cared for by her father, who worked regular hours, and an au pair. When Millie was 4 her parents separated and Millie remained living with her father. Her mother was an inconsistent and unreliable visitor. Her father felt unconcerned about this as, 'Millie's not used to seeing much of her mother, nothing has really changed for her in that respect.'

It may sound paradoxical to say the less Millie saw of her mother before the divorce, the more she needed to see her after the family split up. Children who have a warm, close and consistent contact with their parents absorb an internal picture of the parent and their relationship with them – 'Mummy in my heart and I can ask her questions' – as one child described it. When parent and child are separated, the child has the potential to enjoy a life independent of the parents, because there is a sense in which he carries the parent with him inside, giving a sense of support and security. Where there has been a less good relationship, the child may have a fragile sense of 'mummy in my heart'. They may feel they don't really know the parent enough to hold on to them in absences and need frequent contact to strengthen the relationship.

Fun together or a waste of time?

For a child, the most worrying feeling can be that parents regard time spent with them as a waste of time. Children will quickly construe cancelled arrangements as the parent having something better to do. Dora, with whom this chapter opened, frequently overheard her mother refusing invitations on the basis of 'Well, I've got the children.' Dora slowly built up a picture of a mother who would rather be accepting social invitations but was constrained to spend time with her children. A vulnerable child may be quick to construe 'I have to go to work' for 'I don't want to be with you.'

Go to sports day!

Parents' interest in the child's life outside home leads to a sense of pride, achievement and validation. In the general run of things, children can withstand parents not always being able to attend events such as sports day or prizegivings. However, after a divorce, a concrete way of showing children they are still the centre of the parent's life is to place extra emphasis on such attendances. The highlight of Dora's young life was when her father flew from a business meeting in Leeds to Bournemouth in order to hear her play the recorder in a school concert.

Sharing the Care – Coping with Two Homes

'I live with my mum from Monday to Thursday and then I go to my dad. It's okay, I just have to remember where I am.'

'Remember where you are?'

'Yep, it's okay, I see both my parents but, like, my mum likes everything tidy, and my dad doesn't care, so I have to remember to clear my stuff up at my mum's.'

'During the week I live with my mum and then at the weekend I live with my dad and that's all right but sometimes I forget to take things.'

'I want to go on holiday with my dad but my mummy's having a big birthday party and my mum says it's okay I can choose what I do but I can't choose, 'cos I don't want to let my mum or my dad down.'

There are many advantages of shared custody. Children are encouraged to move between two separate families, helping to diminish the sense of loss which accompanies divorce. Children are encouraged to have maximum involvement and contact with both parents and the parents may endeavour to continue a joint upbringing of the child and to be flexible in times of one parent's difficulty or illness.

> Shared custody is usually a result of both parents actively wanting the children in their homes.

Going to daddy because it is 'his turn' or 'to give mummy a rest' is quite a different feeling from 'my dad gets excited because I'm coming, and my mum always stays in Sunday nights 'cos I'm home again.' However, even in the most well managed households shared custody children may need help with the potentially disturbing feelings of being perpetually on the move.

♦ Children can be helped to trust both environments by

having their own room or special place in both homes.

◆ Ideally, possessions should be left in both bases, so that the child has the minimum sense of 'being like my bag, I'm carried from place to place.' Children may be confused at first at what should be kept where, and may initially do a lot of chopping and changing. It can be complicated for the parents, but what is important is that the child has an evolving sense of what goes where in their life.

◆ A 10-year-old found packing a suitcase every weekend almost intolerable in its symbolism of her split life. A very different experience from the child who says 'and then when I go into my bedroom, and I see my duvet and stuff, I know that I've been away but everything is still the same here.' Such a child is likely to feel more in control of their life.

Playing parents off against each other

At some time or another all children will attempt to play one parent against the other, to their own advantage. Shared custody provides a potential minefield in this area.

Children will try to manipulate parents for their own ends, 'Daddy says I can' or 'Daddy lets me.' They may also learn very quickly that one way of looking after their parents is to tell them what they want to hear about the other parent.

Dora's mother was extremely jealous of Dora's step-mother, feeling that the father provided much better materially for this wife than he had done for her. In times of stress she would ply Dora, on return from visits, with questions about her step-mother's possessions. Dora quickly learnt that if she said that Joan had a new dress her mother would be distressed, and so she began to think of more acceptable answers, such as, 'Daddy and Joan had a row 'cos Joan wanted a new dress.' Whilst this response decreased her mother's distress, it fuelled her mother's ever-present rage against her father, and made Dora feel both powerful and frightened in her relationship with her parents.

There may very well be different rules and expectations in the two homes, especially if there are step-parents involved. In life children are adapting all the time to different authorities; home, school, youth club, etc. Whilst children may seek to exploit the two different regimes, it can provide parents with a superb opportunity to show children that there is more than one way of doing things. 'But daddy lets me have supper in front of the TV.'

'Well, that's fine, daddy lets you but I won't. It doesn't mean he's right and I'm wrong, or I'm right and he's wrong, it just means we're different.'

Remarriage

'Daddy's going to marry Clare, it's the pits, it's the absolute pits, that's the end', sobbed one tearful 9-year-old whose parents had been separated for four years. He went on to voice his belief that one day his parents would have been reunited and that the impending remarriage had shattered this belief. Such a hope for some children can become almost a purpose for living.

It is important for parents to take on board the significance of a remarriage. At this moment some children may face for the first time the irrevocable truth that adults have known for many years. On the other hand, a remarriage which takes place quickly after a separation can lead children to feeling a grudge against the new spouse. The fantasy is that their parents would have got back together some day, had this new person not come along.

> It can be helpful for step-parents dealing with such hostilities to remember that it is not them personally that the hostility is aimed at, it is them as a phenomenon. The step-parent is a constant reminder to the child that their parents have separated.

Introducing the step-family gradually will give the child time and space to think, as well as feel, about what has happened to them. However, remarriage is 'adult business', and I was slightly amused by a couple who sought my advice on how they should tell the husband's children they were going to get married.

'We had thought of asking them if it was all right if we got married.'

'And what will you do if they say no?'

If children can attend, or even take part in, the second wedding it can lead them to feel that they are going to be a significant part of their parent's future life.

On Being Adult

I would like to leave the ending of this chapter to Tom's parents. On one visit they were describing the complexities of sharing the care of their two children. They were explaining how it had been much easier when both children were under 6 and didn't have their own independent social lives. They were describing painfully, and in some ways resentfully how, as the children were growing up, they had agreed that the children's social life should take priority over theirs.

So if Tom was invited to a birthday party on a Saturday when he was supposed to be visiting his father, then Tom would not be put in the position of having to choose. Rather the father would make it his responsibility to get Tom to the party. Potentially this caused a huge disruption in the parents' lives and a degree of acrimony with their respective new partners. However, as Tom's mother said, 'We have chosen to separate, and we must take the responsibility and help the children to cope with the consequences of our decision. They did not choose for us to separate, and we want to keep their lives going in as regular and normal a way as possible. Our child-care arrangements work, but they work because the adults work very hard to make it work.'

'Above all,' said Tom's father, 'we feel they should never have to choose between us. We try very hard to be co-operative and flexible in making our arrangements, even if sometimes we do it between gritted teeth.'

> It is so easy for parents, maybe stressed and unhappy themselves, to be drawn into childlike confrontations with each other, particularly around arrangements for the children. Children always and inevitably bring out the child in their parents.

Believing in Goodness

And to Dora, who you will remember opened this chapter with her lack of belief in goodness. She was a deeply unhappy child who vowed she would never marry, ''Cos I don't want my children to know about divorce.' After a prolonged period of help she said one day, 'You know, when my mum and dad split up it felt all jagged, and I didn't like anybody...now... it's getting smooth and liking again.'

'And why do you think that is?'

''Cos I tell you (how I feel)...and you helped mummy and daddy to understand and I thought they didn't.'

Summary

- ◆ The task for parents in divorce is to help children to make the best of it, to keep alive the fact of the separation and yet not let it spoil everything.
- ◆ It is almost impossible to give parents any support in remaining together as a parental couple, as opposed to a sexual couple, without increasing their guilt and anxiety about the children. Offering help in remaining together as a parental couple can imply that it was not in the children's interests for them to split up.
- ◆ In divorce, families have to find out how they want to be together, and the ways in which this can be managed.
- ◆ Marriages do not fail, they begin, usually with high hopes and expectations, they evolve, usually with a fair degree of chaos, and they end, sometimes prematurely and unexpectedly by death or divorce.
- ◆ It may not be possible to avoid painful disappointment during divorce, but there are other ways of thinking about divorce than success or failure.
- ◆ Telling the children together will reinforce the idea that parents may be intending to stay together as 'a parental couple', if not as lovers.
- ◆ In trying to explain to children why parents are separating, it is usually best to be as honest as possible and as simple as possible.
- ◆ In order to make sense of emotional experiences, children need to be told the facts.

◆ No reason will be good enough in your children's minds for you to divorce.

◆ It will not make sense to your child that you love him but do not want to live with him.

◆ It is important to tell children that you know they cannot understand why this is happening, and to acknowledge and hold their feelings of panic and bewilderment.

◆ Your child's predominant thought will be: 'What will happen to me now?'

◆ Children need parents to stress as far as possible that the divorce 'is not your fault, it is nothing to do with you, this is adult business.'

◆ Never ask your child to choose between their parents.

◆ Children cannot be expected to think rationally when their whole world has been turned upside down. Sometimes it is most helpful not to offer explanations but simply to accept how the child feels.

◆ There are as many ways of reacting to divorce as there are children.

◆ One child may carry all the pain and grief for the family.

◆ After divorce, children need to be encouraged to establish a new way of having a relationship with the departed parent.

◆ Children under 3 need to consolidate their sense of security by being able to sequence and predict their daily lives.

◆ Children 4 to 7 years old are likely to blame themselves for their parents' divorce.

◆ Children between 8 and 11 years old may have a predominant sense of rage and injustice.

◆ Children over 12 years are more capable of verbalising their feelings than younger children, and are likely to show more overt grief and loss.

◆ Feelings are not all that children have to negotiate in divorce. There is often loss of social status and finance.

◆ Do not draw children into adult conflicts.

◆ Do not mix facts and feelings. Some parents find it more straightforward to make arrangements with each other in writing.

◆ Access visits should be reliable and consistent.

◆ The less good the child's relationship with the departed parent before the divorce, the more the child needs to see the parent after the divorce.

◆ Some children may worry that parents regard time spent with them as a waste of time.

◆ Support your child's outside interests, for example go to sports day!

◆ Children need to feel welcome and wanted in both homes.

Mothers who work outside the home can feel that they end up doing neither mothering nor their paid work properly.

On Never Winning – a Word to Working Mothers and Fathers

'I know now I'll never win...if he has problems it's because of the childminder. If he does well, it's because of the childminder.'

(New mother returning to work.)

'I'm torn in two. I love my kids, I love my job. I can't stay at home, we need the money, I'd go mad, but I end up feeling I don't do anything properly. I can't win.'

(Working mother with three children.)

'We share the chores, we've worked it all out. We work it out every Sunday evening. But when the stress is on, my job comes second and he opts out of home. It's just presumed it's my job really to run the home. He's the main breadwinner, so what can I do? I can't win.'

(Working mother)

Change and Opportunity

If we believe what we read, it was all so easy in the 1950s. Dad went out to work, mum stayed at home and looked after the house and children. When dad came home, mum cooked a meal and the family sat around the dining room table sharing their day. Then dad read his paper while mum washed up. Everyone was happy. Or so we are told. Those of us raised in the 1950s may have other thoughts.

A young father was telling me of a row with his own father who was watching him bath his baby son. A conversation had begun about the young man's 'hands-on' involvement in his child's daily care and, as is the way with families, an argument began as the new father complained bitterly about the

131

grandfather's lack of involvement in his life as a child.

'For instance,' he said, 'I don't ever remember you bathing me, you just used to come upstairs to stay goodnight when mum told you to.'

'I wasn't allowed to bath you.'

'What?'

'I wasn't allowed, it wasn't done...of course I wanted to, but it was your mother's job.'

Maybe parenting was easier in one way when each parent had a prescribed role. But that says nothing of the frustrations and disappointments felt by each partner. These frustrations may not even have been thought about, let alone expressed.

A lively 78-year-old grandmother, very much the matriarch of her family, was watching TV coverage of the first woman in space. She caused much amusement in the family by suddenly bursting out: 'Oh, what a time girls have today! If I had had those opportunities...oh, what I could have done if I'd been born a young woman today.'

The fact is that fifties fathers may have been frustrated at being kept distant from their children. Fifties mothers may have felt frustrated by being kept tied to the home. Both sexes would have found it difficult to complain about their lot without feeling 'a bad parent'.

The Impact of Choice

'The past is another country, they do things differently there.' (*The Go-Between*, L P Hartley)

As we have already discussed in previous chapters, family life is now far more fluid. There are single parents who go out to work full-time, and part-time. Both parents may go out to work full-time. One parent may work full time, one part time. Fathers go out to work, while mothers stay at home. Mothers go out to work, while fathers stay at home. One or both parents may now work from home. Sharing the care of the children and household chores is much more common nowadays. Employers may find themselves in a 'double bind'. On one hand they have become much more 'family friendly'. On the other hand, it sometimes seems as though employers have become more demanding and encourage people to work more than they should. We are now also having reports of a growing resentment of child-free couples that they are having to work longer hours or antisocial hours, to cover for employers' family friendly policies. Roles and choices available to both sexes are much more complex. Whilst such choices bring freedom, they also bring complications and tensions. Some parents, maybe particularly mothers, trying 'to have it all', often end up feeling that they have nothing.

Where there is no choice

Of course for some mothers there is no choice about working lucratively. They may be a sole provider or the family may need a second income, either to keep their heads above water or to raise their standard of living. Parents in such a situation may be pleased to be providing some income but may also feel frustrated and resentful at not being able to give the children what they feel they really need.

'We were so poor as kids... but we were rich, we got so much love and attention. But I can't give mine that. I know I should, but I'm so tired at the end of the day. It is really hard to start another job at 6 o'clock – listening to them and giving them attention – however much I love them.'

Just a Housewife – Should Mothers be Paid?

Of course, mothers work all the time. Mothers do not decide 'to return to work' after childbirth. It can be argued that the decision is whether or not to extend your working hours by taking on a job outside the home. Like it or not, we live in a society in which we seem to equate value with financial reward. The more important someone's job in society's eyes, the more they are likely to be paid. Many mothers have to work. Others choose to work. Others may not be able to feel enough self-worth doing the job of mothering, which is unpaid.

'I'm just a housewife.'

'Oh, I just look after the kids.'

Implicit in comments like these is: 'I'm of no real value.' If mothers were paid for mothering, would the 'just a mother' feeling go away?

Pause for thought

- ◆ How do you want your children to describe you as parents when they are your age?
- ◆ If you were not working outside the home, how would your life be different? How would you organise your time?

Doing Neither Well

The quotations at the beginning of this chapter illustrate common phenomena among working mothers, i.e. the feeling of 'not winning'. What is the battle that is trying to be won? Mothers may feel guilty if they enjoy their work and are glad to be out of the home. They may feel guilty if they do not really want to work outside the home, but it is a financial necessity.

Maybe what is not being won is the status of 'super parent'. The idea is of a mother who manages to combine work and motherhood serenely and competently. At work she is conscientious and efficient, at home she is calm, warm and sympathetic. Of course, such 'super parents' do exist. However, without very high incomes affording help of an excellent quality, for most women the struggle to keep all the balls in the air becomes a nightmare.

> 'I'm not so much a juggler, more a Greek plate smasher.'
> *(Exhausted working mother.)*

A good enough mother

Winnicott has written that no child needs a perfect mother. All a child needs is a 'good enough mother'. There is a big difference between being 'good enough' and 'perfect'. Your ability to cope with this discrepancy will depend very much on how you feel about your own competence and disappointment. The last thing a busy working mother needs to do is to beat herself up for not being super efficient. Accept that you are doing your best, that you can't be perfect, and you don't have to be. When you feel you've got it wrong, talk to the children. Explain that, however it feels to them, they are not the problem or at fault. Explain to the children that you want to give them your time and attention, and are disappointed when you feel tired after work and become irritable with them. Sometimes drawing a vicious circle with the children will help.

Mum home tired from work

You think it's your fault

Mum pleased to see you

Mum gets cross with you

You are pleased to see mum and want her time and attention

Mum gets cross with herself

Mum gives you time and attention

Mum begins to hurry and feels sad and disappointed about hurrying you

Mum tired and knows lots more jobs to do

Quality Time – or a Bag of Crisps?

We all benefit from individual time during which another person focuses on our needs and interests. The idea of 'quality time' in which parents spend short periods of time focused on their children has grown up as a solution to the hurly-burly days in the lives of most working parents. It has, of course, many advantages. Parents may feel relieved of their guilt of 'not doing either thing properly' and the children will thrive on having their parents preoccupied with nothing but them for a spell.

However, is 'quality time' what children really need? Perhaps one of the advantages of the fifties home was that mother was likely to be available to children 'on demand'. Children would be getting on with their activities, and she would be getting on with household chores. But mother and child had instant access to each other. Perhaps what children most need are parents available to them, to focus on their interests and needs, *when they want them to*. As one mother said: 'She treats me like a bag of crisps, she dips into me when she feels like it.' Some working mothers may feel stressed by such a comment, others may feel relieved that they don't always have to be planning quality time.

Of course it may suit children to have mother on demand, but mothers can't have children on demand. Some children do bully their mothers. They don't mean to bully, they are simply trying to get their needs met in order to survive. Hugh Jolly helped mothers to feel less bullied by their children by refusing to use the phrase 'feeding on demand', changing it to 'on request'.

From the Child's Point of View

'My mum really likes work'

Children quickly get into a muddle. If parents have to spend a lot of time on work, particularly at evenings or weekends when the child is around, then the child may form the conclusion that mum would rather work than be with me. Children are not open, on the whole, to reasonable discussions about why parents must have other preoccupations than them. The feeling is likely to be that if mum and dad liked me they would want to be with me.

◆ It is important to explain to your children, when you are not able to spend much time with them because of work commitments, that you too are disappointed. Give a simple, factual explanation of the work situation. Focus on how disappointing it is for you both not to be able to spend time together. Give the children something to look forward to – but be realistic. Do not promise to take them to the cinema next Saturday unless you are very sure the work pressures will be over by then. While you are waiting for the treat, throw into the conversation: 'I'm really looking forward to next Saturday when we are going to the pictures together.'

The parental child

It is inevitable in most busy households that a responsible

child, usually the oldest child, will be relied upon to take on some of the minor household chores. Whilst it is important that all in a family take their fair share of responsibility, it is not helpful if a responsible child becomes 'a prop' for the working parents. No childhood is perfect, but children who become substitute parents to younger children can feel robbed of any childhood. Making one child responsible for the others may also upset the balance in a family. The older child may feel burdened and resentful, which may result in bullying of the younger children. It may be much better not to leave one child in charge, but to leave all the children with specific tasks and responsibilities.

There's Nothing Wrong with Not Coping

Exhaustion seems to be an occupational hazard of parenting!

The exhausted parent

A mother once described herself to me as 'an eternal honeypot'. She felt that she had to go on doling out sweetness in spoonful after spoonful, all day every day. We all know that the more spoonfuls you take out of a honeypot, the emptier it becomes. An exhausted parent can be a real source of worry to a child. Again, the child is likely to construe your exhaustion as their fault. They may well misconstrue your exhaustion as lack of interest in them, or distaste for them. You owe it to your family to look after yourself, but most of all, you owe it to yourself.

> Parenting may involve self-sacrifice, but it should not equate with it.

The more exhausted you become, the more disenchanted with life you are likely to become.

◆ When you are exhausted, explain to your children that it is not their fault, and that they are not expected to remedy it. Explain to them how you are going to remedy it. For example, 'I'm going to have an early night tonight.'

◆ There is a difference between making children feel they have to cure your exhaustion, and enabling them to feel that they can help. 'I'm worn out, working all day, and looking after you kids,' is very different from, 'I know I'm snapping at you. I'm very tired, and what would help us to have a better time together would be if you would help me to load the dishwasher,' etc.

◆ There is nothing wrong with not coping... there is nothing wrong with not coping even if it feels there is everything wrong with it. Everybody gains in a family if mother looks after herself. One of the most difficult tasks of being a mother is to remember to mother yourself. Sometimes feeling you are 'not coping' is a way of sending a message to other members of the family that 'I need looking after as well.'

◆ High expectations are all well and good – if you can keep to them relatively easily.

◆ Don't feel guilty if you 'can't get it all done' – nobody can. There is a limit to what any one person can take on, and you will do more some days than others. There is nothing wrong with not coping.

On Planning to Be a Working Mother

Balancing home and work demands is likely to go more smoothly if you plan as much as possible in advance. There is always going to be the unforeseen to cope with, but making as many safety nets as possible can help to reduce tensions. The secret seems to lie in careful planning, but somehow being able to maintain enough mental flexibility to allow your plans to be disrupted. As one mother said: 'We can cope when plan A doesn't work, we can cope when plan B doesn't work, it's when we get to plan F we start to panic.'

> Before returning to work, list your priorities as a family. What order would you place such things as money, time together, expensive treats and holidays etc? How are you going to maintain these priorities?

◆ How are you going to balance 'home work' with 'job work'? Think about how you are going to manage daily chores such as meals, shopping, school runs, etc. What happens when the children are ill, when one of you is ill, when there is an unexpected school closure for a day? For a week?

◆ Realistically there are bound to be frustrations and disappointments if you are both working outside the home full-time. Being realistic about that fact can be a great relief. Accept that, from time to time, one or both of you are going to feel upset and put upon. Balancing parenthood and work is bound to involve compromise.

◆ Don't involve the children in your resentments. 'I've worked all day long but your dad will never load the dishwasher' is not helpful. Your child will only feel that they have got to take sides or become 'a parent to the parent' – 'Mum works so hard for us, I feel sorry for her. I try to help her by keeping the others quiet and things but...'

◆ If you are working at home, does a parent on the premises mean instant access for the family? Both children and partner may find it difficult to adjust to the idea that a mother working at home has to maintain strict boundaries around her work. Because she is in the house, it doesn't necessarily mean that she is available. Equally, a mother working outside the home with a partner working at home, may find it hard to tolerate his boundaries. It may not be appropriate for him to leave his work to be able to sort out a fight between the children.

◆ Who is going to take responsibility for looking after your relationship – making time for each other, for a social life, and purely adult activities? This may be particularly important where both parents have full-time jobs. Your priorities are likely to be your children and your job, and 'couple time' is likely to become a scarcity unless it is planned.

◆ Single working mothers need to plan where and how they are going to get their adult support and social life.

A Beauty Queen with a Briefcase

A 7-year-old tomboy was struggling with her feelings that 'boys get a better deal than girls.' With two strong, attractive and clever, much older, brothers, she saw few advantages in being the girl in the family. Her father had a glamorous, and exciting job and she was something of a bully to her somewhat gentle-natured mother. Things began to change when her mother eventually found employment outside the family home. Several months later, on returning from the first family holiday, she drew a picture of her mother in a bikini, holding a briefcase. 'My mum is a lady, she goes to work,' she wrote.

Advantages of a working mother

Both parents and children are likely to be ambivalent about mother working outside the home. However, as this little girl discovered, it can provide children with an opportunity to see their mother as an independent person, who can do other things as well as mothering. By providing children with such a role model, it is possible that the working mother may encourage girls, in particular, to grow up and achieve adult skills. Girls are offered a broader spectrum in their future as a woman and may realise very early on that there are many ways of being a woman. Of course, such a thought is more likely to be helpful to a child at say 6 to 7 years old, than at 6 to 7 months old.

Having Fun Together

When you decided to have children you thought it would be fun. The risk in families is that children have fun, and adults have fun with children. What can get lost is the idea of adults having fun together. In the hurly burly of family and working life, it seems as though the highest casualty is time alone for you as parents. Part of your planning in returning or continuing to work after the arrival of the children must include the question: 'Who is going to look after our relationship?' Couples have to choose what they are going to look after. How this is arranged will differ from couple to couple. It is simply a question of ensuring that you have time together to do what you genuinely enjoy doing together. It is also a question of having time for solo projects. By one of you taking responsibility for planning your time together, be it arranging a babysitter, or simply noticing what is on at the local cinema, or planning a dinner party or an evening at the pub, time together will be ensured. The paradox is that by one of you taking responsibility for this, the other is somehow freed to also come up with ideas.

And what should adults do with their time alone, and what should they talk about? So often parents will tell me that when they do have time alone, they spend it talking about the children in their absence! Of course, it is important to share focused thought and attention on your children. However, it is also important to give focused thought and attention to looking after each other, as opposed to the family as a whole.

Single Parents

This chapter has been written very much from the viewpoint of mothers within a couple deciding to return to work. Of course, all the points raised are equally applicable to lone mothers – and fathers. Single parents tell me that one of the most difficult aspects of their lives is finding adult support for themselves and the time, and sometimes the effort, to enjoy adult company.

Summary

- Roles within the family are more fluid today than in previous generations.
- Mothers who have to work outside the home for financial reasons may feel frustrated and resentful at not being able to give their children the emotional support they feel they could give if they were a full-time mother.
- Would mothering be more valued if it were paid?
- Winnicott has written that no child needs a perfect mother. All a child needs is a 'good enough' mother.
- There is nothing wrong with not coping.
- If you feel you are not coping, explain to your children that it is not their fault, and that you do not expect them to put it right.
- Do children need 'quality time' or do they need parents they can 'dip into' as and when they want – or do they need both?
- If you are preoccupied with work, the children may be

afraid that you would rather be working than with them.

◆ A reliable older child may be given too much responsibility if both parents are absent from the home.

◆ Parenting may involve self-sacrifice, but it should not equate with it. Make time for yourself.

References

Introduction

Lusseyran, J., *What One Sees Without Eyes* (Floris Books, 1999).
Shakespeare, W., *Henry V.*
Dasheu S. and L., *Mariner's Weather Handbook* (Beowulf Inc, Arizona, USA, 1998).
The Concise Oxford Dictionary of Current English (Oxford @ The Clarendon Press).
Winnicott, D. W., *The Child, the Family and the Outside World* (Harmondsworth: Penguin Books, 1984).

Chapter 1

Phillips A., *Personal Communication* (1988); *On Kissing, Tickling and Being Bored* (Faber & Faber, 1993).

Chapter 2

Leach, P., *Your Baby and Child* (Penguin Books, 1997).
Winnicott, D. W., *The Child, the Family and the Outside World* (London, Tavistock, 1957).

Chapter 3

Winnicott, D. W., *Deprivation and Delinquency* (Tavistock, Routledge, 1990).
Klein, M., *Envy and Gratitude* (Hogarth Press, 1975).
Bowlby, J., *The Making and Breaking of Affectional Bonds* (Routledge, 1994).

Chapter 4

Shakespeare, W., *The Tempest.*
Winnicott, D. W., *Deprivation & Delinquency* (Tavistock, 1990).

Chapter 5

Ainsworth, N. D. S. and Wittig, B. A., 'Attachment and Exploratory Behaviour of One Year Olds in a Strange Situation' in B. W. Foss, (ed.) *Determination of Infant Behaviour* IV, London: Methuen (1969).

Williams, Y., *Personal Communication* (1998).

Eigen, M., personal communication to Adam Phillips.

Winnicott, D. W., *The Family and Individual Development*, Tavistock Publications (1968).

Shakespeare, W., *King Lear, The Tempest.*

Phillips, A., personal communication (1990).

Edgecombe, R., 'The Border Between Therapy and Education', lecture delivered to The Forum For The Advancement of Educational Therapy, June 22 1977.

Keenan, B., *An Evil Cradling* (Vintage, 1993)

Chapter 6

Shakespeare, W., *Hamlet.*

Cox, M., personal communication.

Chapter 7

Jolly, H., personal communication.

Winnicott, D. W., *The Maturational Processes & the Facilitating Environment* (H. Karnac, 1990).

Further Reading

Chapter 1

Skynner and Cleese, *Families and How to Survive Them* (Mandarin Paperbacks).

Clare, S., *Releasing your Child's Potential* (Pathways, How To Books, 2000)

Haslam, D., *Stress Free Parenting – How to Survive the 0–5s* (Vermilion Books, 1998).

Biddulph, S., *The Secret of Happy Children* (Thorsons, 1998).

Chapter 2

Erickson, E. H., *Childhood and Society* (Penguin Books, 1969). (Chapters 6 and 7 may be particularly useful.)

Chapter 3

Clare, S., op. cit. (Chapter 6 – 'Disciplining or Devastating Your Child' may be particularly helpful.)

Biddulph, S., op. cit. (Chapters 4 and 5 may be particularly helpful).

Chapter 4

Brown, K., *Bullying – What Can Parents Do?* (Monarch, 1997).

Lawson, S., *Helping Children Cope with Bullying* (Sheldon, available from Kid Scape).

Elliot, M., *Feeling Happy, Feeling Sad* (Hodder & Stoughton, 1991). (For children 2–6 years old.)

Elliot, M., *101 Ways to Deal with Bullying* (Hodder & Stoughton).

Elliot, M., *Willow Street Kids* (DE (UK)/PA, 1992).

Chapter 5

Freud, S., *Psychoanalysis for Teachers and Parents* (The Pelican Freud Library, Penguin Books, Harmondsworth, Middlesex).

Chapter 6

Ayolan, O. and Flasher, A., *Chain Reaction – Children and Divorce* (Jessica Kingsley, 1993).

Chapter 7

Haslam, D., *Stress Free Parenting* (Vermillion, 1998).
Wilson, T., *Working Parents Companion* (NCT, 1999).

Useful Addresses

The Anti-Bullying Campaign
185 Tower Bridge Road
London SE1 2US.
Tel: (020) 7378 1446

Parents Network
Room 2
Winchester House
Kennington Park
11 Cramner Road
London SW9 6EJ.
Tel: (020) 7735 1214

House Husband Link
(Aims to promote contact between men who care for child and home.)
PO Box 636
Thornton Heath
Surrey CR7 8TQ.

One Parent Families in Scotland
(Providing advice, information and support groups for lone parents, separated parents, and lesbian and gay parents.)
13 Gayfield Square
Edinburgh EH1 3NX.
Tel: (0131) 556 3899.

Index

anger/angry, 11, 13, 33, 52, 76, 106, 119, 120

boarding school, 42–43
boundary/ies, 2, 10–12, 64, 73, 82, 96, 139
Bowlby, J., 63
bullying, 68–82

child care, 127
comfort/ing/ed, 65, 97
communication, 3, 4, 5, 10–11, 20, 40, 55, 66, 76–77, 81, 86, 94, 95
confidence, 28, 38
conflict, 18–19, 21, 23, 28, 30, 85, 118
coping, 86, 124, 137, 138, 141

defiance, 73–74
depression, 94
development, 30, 54–55, 65, 91, 112
divorce, 27, 28, 100–130, 140

envy, 44, 46–48, 58, 66
expectations, 12–14, 16–17, 19, 28, 30–33, 85, 89, 125, 138

families, 9, 10, 21, 23–25, 30, 33, 44, 74, 77, 90, 100, 102, 132–133, 138
father, 9, 25, 47, 78, 102, 119, 131, 132

gloating, 43
grandparents, 15–16
guilt, 3, 49, 61, 80, 108, 120, 128, 134– 135, 138

jealousy, 41, 44, 47, 50

Leach, P., 34
learning, 45, 59, 89, 90–93, 95, 99
lying, 52–57

monster/s, 39, 40, 41
mother, 25, 89, 131–140

Phillips, A., 8, 10
play, 78, 95
praise/d, 57

remarriage, 126–127
rivalry, 32, 33–34, 44, 47, 48, 49

schooling problems 83–100
secure base, 89, 90, 91, 94, 95, 100–102
self-esteem, 90
single parent, 10, 21, 27, 141
smacking, 10–11
spoiling, 38–39, 58, 64
stealing, 62–67
stress: children, 60–61
stress: parents, 20, 79

temper/tantrum/s, 26, 86

Winnicott, D., 4, 6, 18, 63, 81, 134, 141
working mothers, 131–142